Thimble
of Soil

Thimble of Soil

A Woman's Quest for Land

Linda K. Hubalek

Butterfield Books Inc.
Lindsborg, Kansas

Thimble of Soil
© 1996 by Linda K. Hubalek
Fifth Printing 2000
Printed in the United States of America

For details and order blanks for the *Butter in the Well* series, the *Trail of Thread* series, and the *Planting Dreams* series, please see page 103 in the back of this book. If you wish to contact the publisher or author, please address Butterfield Books, Inc., PO Box 407, Lindsborg KS 67456. Each book is $9.95, plus $3.00 s/h for the first book ordered and $.50 for each additional book.

Consulting Editor: Dianne Russell
Cover Design: Jody Chapel, Cover to Cover Design
Cover photo of Margaret, Salina, and Sarah Kennedy in Ohio, 1854
Maps and photos courtesy of Elinor Corman, Linda K. Hubalek, Kansas State Historical Society, and the Elizabeth M. Watkins Community Museum
Quilt design used on cover: Sawtooth Star

Publisher's Cataloging in Publication
(Prepared by Quality Books Inc.)

Hubalek, Linda K.
Thimble of soil : a woman's quest for land / Linda K. Hubalek.
-- Aurora, Colo. : Butterfield Books, 1996.
p. cm. -- (Trail of Thread ; 2)
Includes bibliographical references.
SUMMARY : A family from Ohio becomes involved on the free-state side against proslavery forces in Kansas before the Civil War.
Audience: Age: 9-18.
Preassigned LCCN: 96-83113.
ISBN 1-886652-07-4.
1. Frontier and pioneer life--Juvenile fiction. 2. West (U.S.)--History --Juvenile fiction. 3. Kansas--History--1854-1861--Juvenile fiction. I. Title.

PZ7.H833Thi 1996   813'.54
                             QB196-20115

To the women who fought for Kansas' statehood:

Thank you for not giving up.

God bless these old settlers, these old Kansans, these old pioneer wives. We women really thought you were not going to give us a chance for our lives. We have gone through just as much as any of you. As the alpine traveler, when he gets down to the foot, can stop and look back and glance over the path and see the perilous places he has passed through, and the deep dangers he has escaped in more than one instance in safety, so we can look back now and see what great difficulties we have passed through in our early days. My mind goes back with lightning rapidity through twenty-five years past, and takes in what has been wrought here.

In 1854 we christened Kansas, and oh! I remember it well. Everybody seemed to be enthused with the spirit of freedom's crusade. We mothers have passed through a trying ordeal, but we can look back over the ground with a swell of pride in our hearts when we think of the glorious results.

—*The Kansas Memorial*, 1880

Books by Linda K. Hubalek

Butter in the Well
Prärieblomman
Egg Gravy
Looking Back
Trail of Thread
Thimble of Soil
Stitch of Courage
Planting Dreams
Cultivating Hope
Harvesting Faith

Acknowledgments

I would like to express my sincerest thanks to all of the people who helped with *Thimble of Soil*, especially my newfound Kennedy, Curless, and Pieratt "cousins." Thank you very much for your time and devotion to the project.

Linda Katherine Johnson Hubalek

Table of Contents

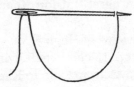

1855 Connection of Main Characters

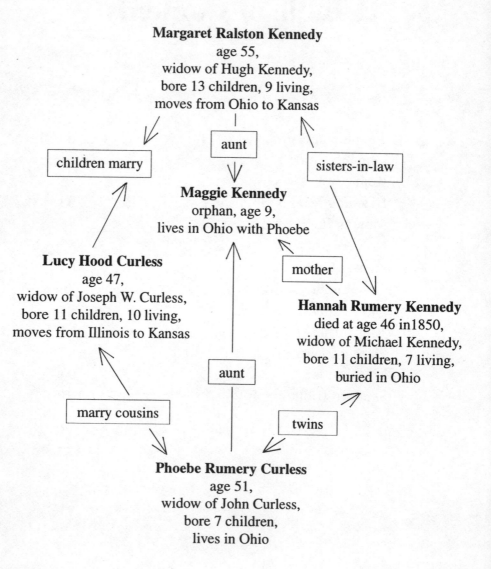

Margaret Ralston Kennedy
age 55,
widow of Hugh Kennedy,
bore 13 children, 9 living,
moves from Ohio to Kansas

children marry

aunt

sisters-in-law

Maggie Kennedy
orphan, age 9,
lives in Ohio with Phoebe

Lucy Hood Curless
age 47,
widow of Joseph W. Curless,
bore 11 children, 10 living,
moves from Illinois to Kansas

mother

Hannah Rumery Kennedy
died at age 46 in1850,
widow of Michael Kennedy,
bore 11 children, 7 living,
buried in Ohio

aunt

marry cousins

twins

Phoebe Rumery Curless
age 51,
widow of John Curless,
bore 7 children,
lives in Ohio

Thimble of Soil

As I was researching the story of my great-great grand-mother, Maggie Kennedy Pieratt, for the *Trail of Thread* series, her aunt, Margaret Ralston Kennedy, kept popping up in files at museums, libraries, and family records. Reading the accounts and old newspaper clippings, I realized that Margaret Ralston Kennedy played an important role in the development of the territory of Kansas.

Digging deeper into her life, I found out she was a widowed mother of thirteen children who made the trek from Ohio to the Kansas Territory with eight of her children in 1855. Normally this would not have been anything unusual, because thousands of people moved west during that time period. What was unexpected for her, and for many other women, was to get caught between the proslavery and free-state fractions that almost tore the territory of Kansas apart. These battles were a catalyst for the Civil War.

Margaret Ralston Kennedy was dedicated to the causes of the North. She firmly believed that Kansas, the United States, and all its people should be free. While the male members of her family were off fighting for a free state, she held together their families and their homesteads, which were left alone in the midst of the battles.

Margaret would have known my Pieratt ancestors from Kentucky, who are featured in the first book in the *Trail of Thread* series. Through map studies, I know they were neighbors in the new territory, and I found documents and stories that link the two women. For instance, John Pieratt became one of the guardians for Margaret's niece, Maggie, when the young girl moved into the territory.

So how and why did the two families—one from the South, the other from the North—get together and stay friends while these battles were going on? That's why I decided to work Margaret Ralston Kennedy's story in between my two grandmothers. Her story connects the two families together.

I was lucky enough to find two pictures of Margaret in the Elizabeth M. Watkins Community Museum in Lawrence, Kansas—one of Margaret standing in front of her house before she left Ohio, and the other of her in old age. Determination was showing in her eyes in both pictures, prompting me to write her story. To make the book as accurate as possible, I drove to Ohio to see where she lived, then followed the wagon trail route down to Kansas, stopping where Margaret filed her claim.

Deborah Pieratt in *Trail of Thread* starts the story of the women who moved to the Kansas Territory. Margaret Ralston Kennedy's battle for survival while trying to establish a new home link the two families together in the second book, *Thimble of Soil*. The third book, *Stitch of Courage*, features Maggie Kennedy, an orphan who follows her family to Kansas and marries Deborah Pieratt's son, James. After a brief lull of quiet in the state, the Civil War breaks out, initiating danger for everyone.

A note to the relatives of these characters: I tried to exhaust all research sources available to make the story as accurate as possible. But records do conflict at times, so please be aware that some dates, stories, and other historical elements, I decided to use may not correspond with your family notes. Some stories were added to show what the women went through to build their homesteads and survive the times.

Dig in! It's your turn to explore the *Thimble of Soil*.

Leaving Home

June 22, 1854

I turned over the letter that my daughter, Salina, handed me, feeling the weight and hearing the sliding sound of something shifting inside. The letter had been sealed with wax around all the seams of the folded paper instead of just a single dollop of sealing wax to hold the four corners together.

I recognized my oldest son, William Bainbridge's, handwriting. Bridge, as he is called, had written earlier this spring from Illinois that he, my son-in-law Will Curless, and a friend, John Wood, were leaving to ride down through the new territories of Kansas and Nebraska to search for land for our families. He must have mailed this letter from a stop along the way.

I smiled as I broke the seal of the letter and grains of soil filtered out. It was Bridge's way of saying he found land.

I carefully unfolded the letter, wiped the dusty paper off with the corner of my apron, and began to decipher his writing.

Sunday evening, May 21, 1854
Westport, Missouri

Dear Mother,

I hope this letter finds you well, as we are. We have completed our investigation of the new territories and are on our way home to Illinois.

We found an area that will accommodate all the Kennedy and Curless families that want to move. We came across a pocket of land in the eastern part of the Kansas Territory that was to our liking. This valley has a small river called the Wakarusa running through it, thick stands of large timber on its banks thinning out to rich black bottom land, and surrounding bluffs to protect the valley. This peaceful area is large enough to allow each man to have 160 acres of prime land at $1.25 an acre. By law, widows are allowed to buy land, too, if you so desire.

We met a few families, out in the middle of nowhere, getting a jump on the territorial opening. So far there are very few people who have settled that far west into the Kansas Territory.

We've heard rumors that groups from the North and South are organizing parties of people to settle in the Kansas Territory. They want to sway the settlers to vote for or against making it a free state, but I don't think it will become a problem. There is so much land available, there will surely be room for everyone interested in starting a new life there. Besides, with our large group, the area will definitely have a free-state stance.

I propose we move as soon as we can get our supplies and families ready to relocate. I will write more details when we get back to Illinois and discuss it among the families.

We are going through Westport to mail a letter for a woman named Deborah Pieratt, a new Kansas homesteader we met, who was anxious to send a letter back home to Kentucky. You will eventually meet her because she will be your new neighbor.

We look forward to your arrival in Illinois, Mother.

Most Affectionately,

Bridge

In his excitement, he mailed this letter in the bustling town of Westport, hoping it would make its way down the Missouri and up the Mississippi Rivers faster than if he waited until getting back to Illinois to write. I could read the Kennedy dedication to his family and the desire for land between his lines in the letter.

Land and freedom have always been top priorities in the Kennedy family from the beginning. It has been the dream of each generation to own the best land they could find, starting with the first ones who left Ireland for America in the 1700s. First landing on the East Coast, they moved west as land became more settled and unavailable to the next generation of sons. During this century they moved down the river from Pennsylvania to Ohio when some of the family had been deeded land by the government for their participation in the Revolutionary War.

Some of the Kennedy, Curless, and Dutton families forged ahead to western Illinois in the 1830s to log the timber, then farm that area. My older children moved there later because there wasn't land enough here in Ohio for them to start farming.

Bridge moved first in '47, marrying our former neighbor girl, Elizabeth, whose parents, Joseph and Lucy Curless, moved their family to Illinois the year before. Then their son, Will Curless, came back and wed my daughter Nettie, taking her to Illinois that winter. Being exactly one year apart, Nettie and Will always had a special bond while growing up, which I knew would continue in their adulthood. My sons Joe and Scott followed shortly afterward and married Illinois girls. My daughter Cate and her husband, Collins Holloway, moved in '53. My youngest sons, Tom and Leander, are itching to move. Now as my older children start their families, they are looking west again.

Initially there were two reasons I stayed behind. I've always lived in Ohio, and it didn't make sense to leave the state. I owned some Kennedy land and it supported me and the four children still at home. Also, the fresh graves of my husband and four children had a very strong grip on my heart.

It is ironic that this letter should come on my wedding anniversary. It's been nine years since Hugh died. Maybe it is a sign from him telling me it is time to pull up my roots, reunite our remaining nine children, and lead them to a better place where we may all live together again.

An explosion of questions are in my mind as I think about such an enormous undertaking. We'd need enough money to buy land, starter seed, and food supplies, to build houses and out-buildings, not to mention the expense of moving. What will it cost to start a new homestead?

How much money could I get for the farm here in Ohio? This land was supposed to be handed down to Leander. He couldn't own land in Kansas since he isn't twenty-one yet, but I could buy land in my name, then turn it over to him later.

What would Sarah and Salina think of leaving their home and friends?

Sarah, almost twenty-eight, can do as she wants, but I think she would move to stay with the family. She has spent the last ten years teaching school and is ready for something new, for marriage has eluded her.

Salina would have no say in the matter, but how do I soften such a hard move for my shy girl? At thirteen, she's just beginning to blossom into a young lady and notice boys. This uprooting would be hardest on her. How would I help her understand?

We'd be moving to an area that is isolated from the states. Towns and stores will spring up, but it will take time to get these established. Do my children realize we would be out in the wilderness, totally dependent on ourselves for food and shelter? I must trust that our parental upbringing, and the guidance of the Lord's hand, have led my sons to make the right decision.

There would be loneliness for home, friends, and the famil-iar. People and places I've known all my life would disappear from my daily circle. Panic creeps in with my thoughts. Can I let go of the safety of my present situation to a new unknown? After Hugh died, I depended on the older male members of his family and mine for advice. Now I'd be on my own.

I'd be leaving my Ralston clan behind. My parents are gone, but siblings still live in the area. Would I ever see them again?

Can I meet this task? Am I physically strong enough to endure the hardships? Right now I'm in good health, but that will change as I get older. Would I be a burden to the children by going along?

But then again—if I can calm my racing heart to think clearly— I realize it would be my chance to claim my own land, to use my mind, body, and spirit to carve a new place out of virgin soil. Decide what crops and livestock I want to raise, watch a new orchard bud and fruit.

My sons are moving with or without me. And as the next generation is being born to them, I don't want to miss the joy of being a grandmother to those children. I couldn't stand being deprived of such memories.

At age fifty-four, this is my last chance to start over and get out from under the shadow of the past. Better to join the family on the move now than put it off until I'm old, crippled, and unable to stand the journey.

I'm going to start a new life on the plains of Kansas.

March 1, 1855

Take along, sell, or give away? Seems like I've been thinking those words night and day for the past month. I had commenced to go through the household belongings immediately when I first heard from Bridge last summer, but then the trip was postponed and so was the packing.

Cholera crept across Missouri last summer, and I wasn't about to move the family into that. After going through the cholera and white plagues that swept through Ohio in the '40s, I would not risk losing the rest of my family. My sons protested until I reminded them of all the Kennedys who died because of the illnesses. Mass graves in cemeteries filled up fast when whole families died and were buried together.

Nettie's husband agreed with me. In '51 they had an outbreak of cholera in Fulton County, Illinois, and Will buried many neighbors who succumbed to the disease. We finally agreed that other emigrants would wait, too, so all the land in the Kansas Territory wouldn't have been claimed by this spring.

Now we'll leave for Kansas Territory as soon as all the families congregate in Schuyler County, Illinois, and the weather turns more favorable.

Currently we're going through everything we own, packing what we want to take along and getting the rest ready for a sale next week. Farm implements, livestock, and other odd and ends we can't cart across country will give us seed money to start over.

It has been hard to look through things we've accumulated for thirty-five years, realizing each item's beginning, history, and future. Tears come quickly to my eyes when I stop to think of special times certain things were used for.

I stood in the tool shed a long time and held Hugh's hand tools that he used to make coffins for loved ones, automatically feeling his presence and mood. It dawned on me that the rust spots on his hand planer could have been from tears, not rain.

When sorting tack and harness in the dim barn, my sense of smell locked in on the leftover scents of sweet hay, animal manure, and sweaty leather. Favorite animals born and died over the years haunt the stalls. Will I live long enough in Kansas to have my new barn acquire these same comforting smells?

Equipment that made countless rounds in our fields stand idle in a row. I grinned at the thought of the first rows of corn I planted with the planter and team. As a new bride I was determined to help out with the fields as well as the home. Those crooked rows embarrassed me from first sprout in the spring until last ear picked in the fall. After the children started arriving I did little of the farm work until Hugh died, then I was back at it again. I can plant a row as straight as any good man now, so I won't be humiliated in Kansas.

Our freight will be moved from Ohio to Illinois by a teamster wagon company. Tom and Leander will travel with our load to insure it gets to our destination. As it is about a 375-mile journey, they will be leaving right after the sale.

Salina and I are staying behind temporarily because of Sarah. John Neal hastily proposed marriage when he realized Sarah was serious about leaving, and she accepted. I regret they decided to stay in Ohio instead of moving with us, but I'm confident she'll be happy here. She wants her wedding to be at our house, like her sisters' were, so I will postpone my leaving. As soon as she's settled, Salina and I will depart for Illinois.

March 7, 1855

Our time left has been stretched to its limit in getting ready to move, planning a wedding, and getting Sarah's dowry together. Each room of the house has haunted me with memories (and robbed me of time) as I sort through decades of accumulation. I keep thinking, how will I condense a whole house of furniture and belongings into one or two wagon loads?

The upstairs bedrooms were crammed with things the children left behind as they moved into their own homes, because there were younger siblings to wear out their clothes, toys, and books. Special things I've packed for grandchildren, but most will be given away or burned.

When was the last time I moved the dresser in the north room?! I found a little cloth doll, singed and sooty, wedged behind it. Back then, Salina told me she had lost it, but it looks like her and Matilda's antics landed the poor doll in the fireplace for some reason. Apparently the doll was rescued, but they were too scared to confess their crime. If only the walls could talk, I'd hear many stories my children hoped I'd never learn.

The afternoon faded to twilight around me last night as I sat by the window, reading faded pages of childhood books. Each young child had a favorite that he or she had memorized by heart, because the easy book was read out loud so many times. Advanced volumes held bits of their young lives: a note from a friend, a school grade card, feathers, or pressed flowers. I wish I could pack all these books for Kansas, but I'll have to settle for their memories instead.

Outgrown clothing has been handed down so many times that only parts of the material can be used. They will make their last round as pieces in quilt blocks. Rather than pack the garments, we have cut out the sections of good material to bring along. I gave Sarah the buttons and hooks off the discarded garments to use again when she makes her own children's clothing.

The girls couldn't believe their first efforts of stitching that I had tucked in a trunk. Samplers made to practice their stitches show that each girl had a slightly different angle and technique, even though they were all only six when they learned to sew. I can still tell on certain quilts where each girl sat around the quilting frame by her stitching.

Some trunks of linens and bedding I had packed, will be moved over to Sarah's new home instead of going to Kansas. Over the years Sarah has pulled linens out of her trunk to use because she didn't marry young. Now we're in a bind putting her trousseau back together in such a short time.

Phoebe Curless is hosting a quilting party to at least get Sarah's Ohio Rose wedding quilt done before the ceremony. She is putting it in my large quilting frame, which I'll leave for Sarah instead of hauling along. The boys can make me another frame once we get settled in Kansas.

We're swapping some of Sarah's quilt tops she made over the years for some of my newer quilts since we don't have time to quilt the tops before her wedding. Actually that will help with the bulk and weight for our freight anyway. She helped with the State of Ohio and the Yankee Puzzle quilts, so naturally those were her first choices. Sarah wanted the Puss-in-Boots, too, but Salina became adamant that it should go to Kansas with her. I realized after their quarrel that it was the first quilt that Salina and Matilda had worked on together. Being only a year apart in age, they were very close until Matilda died three years ago.

It was hard going through Matilda's sewing basket. I had stashed it away after she died and hadn't looked at it until I came across it this week. A waft of lavender stirred my memories when I lifted the lid. She kept a little sachet bag of sweet herbs in her basket to scent her sewing. Scissors, bobbins of thread, and her thimble were mixed in with little treasures that she had hidden in her basket. Only Matilda knew the significance of the shiny quartz rocks and old coins. I never will.

The quilt block Matilda was working on at the time was still there, her threaded needle caught in the material just like she left it. The cut pieces of fabric for the rest of the blocks were stacked together, ready to stitch next. Her pincushion was full of pins and threaded needles.

I stuck her tiny thimble on my little finger, remembering the first awkward stitches of the hot pad she made me for Christmas when she was six. I smiled also, reminiscing about how she cut the material for her project out of the special bolt of cloth I was saving for the girls' Christmas dresses. It was a plaid material and she wanted the pattern in the middle of the swath, not from the edge. I had to do some ingenious piecing to make their dresses that year.

I debated what to do with Matilda's basket, but like so many other things in this house, I haven't decided its fate yet.

The downstairs started out as one big room, for both living and cooking. The walls are plastered and whitewashed, making the room seem large and spacious. In later years we partitioned off a corner for Hugh's and my bedroom when the upstairs got crowded with children.

The long table and benches, chairs, and cupboards made by Hugh over the years will be sold. The only thing I'm packing from the room is the small round walnut table Hugh made for my wedding present. I will not leave that behind. The legs detach from the top, so it can be packed.

Do I dare pack my china dishes? Or will they be a heavy barrel of broken shards by the time I get to Kansas? It is probably best to leave them in Ohio with Sarah. Over time she'll want to get new china, but these will suffice for her first years. Maybe I'll wrap a few favorite pieces in among the quilts along with my silver.

I'm dividing the kitchen utensils into two groups—what I'll need to use on the overland trip, and what I need to start the new household in Kansas.

Simple tinware will be used for meals on the overland trail. All kinds of pots and pans hang from my ceiling beams near the fireplace, but I'll select only the basic utensils to take with me. Cooking staples must be in unbreakable containers that will keep the food dry and clean on the trail. I still need to figure out how much flour, sugar, coffee, and other rations we'll need to carry with us on our trip from Illinois to Kansas.

The contents of the food cellar could easily fill a wagon. At least, because it's now spring, the supply of food in the cellar is near its lowest capacity. Sacks of dried fruits and vegetables will weigh the least and take up less room in the wagon than the containers of preserves. Because of the cost of freight, crocks and earthen jars will be left behind. Sarah can use some, but she doesn't need, nor does she have the space to store the huge number of containers I collected over the years to feed our big family.

Our corner bedroom doesn't contain much, but I've been putting off going through it. The room still haunts me at times with ghosts of births and deaths. Rarely a night has passed that I haven't thought of the husband and children who died in the bed I was crawling into. My bed was so lonely after Hugh died, that I slept in the rocker beside it for several days until exhaustion won out. Over the years I have learned to concentrate on the children we conceived and cherished instead of the pain of the losses. If one is to survive a loved one's death, one must learn that life just changes, not ends.

I wish I could take my bed, but there are more important things that need to make the journey instead. I can sleep on about anything as long as I have a good mattress and bedding to keep me warm.

I remind myself that dresses can be hung on pegs or left in trunks instead of a clothes cupboard or chest of drawers. These large pieces of furniture must be sold. The quality cherry wood pieces should fetch a handsome price.

Do I have room for my rocker? Tensions and muscles are always soothed in the rocker that has been in my family for three generations. It was the first piece of furniture my grandfather made for his bride. It may be best to leave it with Sarah than chance it becoming kindling elsewhere.

The items in the small wooden box I have on our dresser will definitely travel with us. Besides my meager jewelry, the oak box carved by my father holds mementos I cherish of lost ones. Hugh's cuff links I gave him as a wedding present, and Matilda's tenth birthday locket. Elizabeth's brooch that I had given her on her wedding day. The dark lock of downy-soft hair was from baby Joseph Warren. Mary Ann didn't live long enough to leave me any memories but pain.

Whenever I go through these things, I think of another child I almost lost. Oliver would have drowned in the Ohio River if it hadn't been for General Winfield Scott. He and his troops were on their way to fight in the Mexican War, saw the situation, and pulled my son out of the river. The other boys nicknamed him Scott to commemorate the day, and that's the name he goes by now.

A tiny lump of soil and the worn-thin thimble in the bottom of the box link me to my grandmother's past. The story goes that when my grandmother left her homeland, she scooped a bit of the soil into her thimble and carried it across the ocean to America. I barely remember her giving the soil and thimble to me as a young child, but these items and her stories are what taught me to cherish the land we live on.

What legacy and material articles will I leave my grandchildren, those here in Ohio and those yet to be born in Kansas?

March 20, 1855

Hearing a far away rattle of wheels and high-pitched laughter, I glance out the upstairs bedroom window. They're coming. A wagon piled high with furniture and children just turned up the long drive. The wife on the wagon seat beside her husband points to something ahead, and then turns to the children wedged in the load behind her. They have spied the swing in the old apple tree that Hugh hung years ago for our children. I used to watch the children in that swing from my front windows. I can smell the spring apple blossoms just thinking about it. But I'll never smell that scent again.

The couple was over yesterday with the final payment. We toured the farm then, discussing what they need to know about the place. The young couple was so excited to be moving onto their own place, with a larger house for their family and better land than what they were renting. Their future beamed bright in their faces as they walked over my land.

I kept seeing the past. Together Hugh and I watching our crops flourish in the sunshine or perish in storms; the saplings we planted by the house growing into towering oaks; my little boys running around the house becoming family men with farms of their own in another state. The barn, needing paint, looks as weathered and tired as I feel. This week's memories will stay with me forever.

This morning we moved the last of the furniture and bedding over to Sarah's new place. A week ago she and John were married in my home. It was full of family and friends for the event—and furniture. Now it is a hollow shell, waiting for the new family to fill it with laughter and life.

I wish I could pack up the whole house, farm—and township for that matter—and move it all with me to Kansas. This must have been the feeling that my grandmother had at leaving the land and country she knew. For all I know I'm moving to as foreign a place as she did.

Suddenly, I can't face the new family that is taking over my farm. I hate to seem impolite, but right now I'll break down if I talk to them. And I don't want my sadness to mar their happiness.

John and Sarah are taking us to Hamersville to meet the afternoon stagecoach. The girls are waiting for me outside in John's wagon as I take one last walk through the empty house. Seeing the new family though has shaken me out of my trance of memories, and I move down the stairway and out of the house.

I wave to the family coming up the drive, trying to hold a smile through my tears. Climbing in the wagon, I whisper a hoarse "Let's go" to John. He hesitates on the reins, but I nod my head forward. I can't stop to talk to them. I'm leaving my home of thirty-five years and I have a huge lump in my throat. It's better to leave with my head up while I can.

When we got to the orchard, I was ready to bail out, even though the wagon was picking up speed. Reaching across John, I jerked the reins to a stop myself. Climbing down before anyone could help me, I turned back to the house and stared for a moment, trying to remember the details of the scene before me.

Digging for my handkerchief in my reticule, I felt the little bag of mementos underneath. Remembering Grandmother's words, I pulled her thimble out of the bag and walked to the old apple tree. Kneeling down, I dug the thimble into the moist bare spot under the swing. I packed the earth into the thimble, then tucked it back into my reticule. Then I could leave the home I've loved.

Family members stood waiting as we pulled up to the stage-coach stop in town. My eyes grew moist as I scanned the scene. And for some reason I also saw a mental flash of ghost husbands and children that should also have been with the group. It reminded me of all the dear ones, alive and departed, that I'm leaving behind forever.

I'm not sure when, if ever, I'll see my grandchildren by my eldest daughter again. At least they have a new mother, for Elizabeth's husband remarried my widowed niece, Mary Ann, last year. I'll be able to learn of them through her.

Mary Ann's youngest sister, Margaret Jane, came up to hold my hand as soon as I crawled down from the wagon. We've always had a special bond, for she was named after me. I'll miss my little niece.

Orphaned before she was four, Maggie, as she's called, has been bounced between families for the past five years. Since Mary Ann's house is full with her and Abraham's combined families, Maggie is living with another aunt, Phoebe Curless, her mother's twin sister.

Maggie's mother, Hannah, Phoebe, and I grew up together. Hannah and I married two of the Kennedy brothers. Phoebe married their cousin, John Curless. All three of us were widows at early ages. Then Hannah died and now I'm losing my other best friend by moving to the new territory.

Last week I paid a special visit to Phoebe's house just so I could spend time with Maggie. Tears dribbled down her plump cheeks when I gave her the Cleveland Tulip quilt her mother had helped me stitch. Maggie craves stories of her parents, so I gave her as many details as I could remember about the day we quilted this particular top. She traced the thread around the flower pattern with her finger, wondering out loud if her mother stitched around a particular part.

Maggie is so perplexed about life that I worry if she will ever find permanent peace. She was adamant that she'll move to Kansas one day, too, but I know she'll stay near her siblings, wherever they may live.

Her family has had a rough time since Hannah and Michael died. Maggie's brother, Moses, is currently running their parents' general store in Hamersville, although he's been talking about selling it and moving to Indiana. Her siblings Michael, John, and Caroline live with Moses. Maggie's other older brother, William James, moved with some of my children to Illinois a few years ago. What will happen to Michael and Hannah's children?

With a cloud of dust rolling past, the stagecoach screeched to a stop in front of us. Our travel bags were thrown to the driver, who lodged them into the pile of luggage on top, urging us to get in because he was running late. I was holding back, trying to hug as many people as I could while the stagecoach manager was trying to lift me bodily up through the door. The coach lurched away, knocking us into our seats as it took off down the road. Turning to lean out the window, all I could see through a veil of tears was a group outline of my family, disappearing into the dust of the road.

My life in Ohio is over.

Kennedy Valley

Wednesday, May 3, 1855
Bluff City, Illinois

Dear Phoebe,

Thank you for the letter inquiring about our trip to Bluff City. We have been occupied with packing for the departure to Kansas, so I have not taken the time to write letters until now.

After the cold, jarring stage ride to Cincinnati, we spent the night in a hotel near the train station. After a sleepless night, we boarded the train for Indianapolis, Indiana. Neither of us was ready to get back on the sooty, noisy train the next day, but it was better than staying in the flea-infested bed that we spent the night in. The next leg deposited us two days later in Springfield, Illinois.

I don't recall most of the train ride, my mind being back in Hamersville or on our farm. Pictures without sound kept changing over and over in my mind until they faded away like the dust from the stagecoach. A month later I still see flashes of the day: Sarah waving good-bye, Maggie standing in the middle of the road after the others had turned away from our departing stagecoach, the detailed interior of the stagecoach that I stared at for hours to keep from crying.

We made the trip in under a week's time. It was bitter cold for March, but we didn't run into any rain or snow. We stopped at every town along the train route from Ohio to Illinois, sometimes for only a few minutes, so we didn't have time to get out, or for overnight, when the train stopped.

Bare trees ringed established farms the whole way. As a farmer myself, I was curious of the different styles of houses and

15

barns, what livestock was on the place, the variety of trees in the orchards. I should say I watched the passing scenery when I wasn't occupied about our baggage, meals, leering strangers, or finding safe hotels. Everything is different when you travel without a man for guidance and protection. Exhausted, Salina slept for most of the trip because she felt dizzy when awake.

At Springfield we transferred back to a stagecoach for Bluff City. That was a freezing bumpy ride across the frozen ruts they called a road. Thank goodness you insisted we take your lap quilt at the last moment, or we would have frozen to death that last day. As it was, with lack of sleep, poor food, and cold feet, Salina came down with a bad case of quinsy that she can't seem to shake. Tom, Leander, and our belongings arrived a few days before us, all in good shape.

After I got here and discussed the move with my sons, we changed plans again and split the family caravan into three groups for the trip. Because of Salina's poor health, and a few other reasons, she and I will be here in Illinois until this fall.

The first group went overland with a large herd of cattle and eight wagons. They had to wait until there was sufficient grass along the way for the livestock. The ones going by wagon through Missouri are Joe and Mary with their two children, Nettie and Will with their three, Cate and Collins with Rose, Scott and Louise, and the Lewis Stagger family. Tom, Leander, and Lucy Curless's son, Lafayette, went along to help with the animals.

I went down to Sharp's Landing on the Illinois River yesterday morning in a drizzling rain to see the second group leave. The boys had spent their winters rafting logs down to St. Louis, so they decided to move our supplies down the rivers from Illinois to the Kansas Territory because they knew part of the way. Hugh's father moved the family from Pennsylvania to Ohio down the Ohio River. Why not us, too? Mapping it out, Bridge and Asa Dutton will steer the boat down the Illinois River to the Mississippi until they reach Alton, Illinois, then work up the Missouri River as far as they can get. Elizabeth went along to do their cooking. We loaded farm equipment, seed and grain, household goods, (including Nettie's kitchen step-stove that Will had brought back from a St. Louis logging trip), spinning wheels, looms, trunks of bedding, clothing, chickens, a few hogs, and a year's worth of food provisions. With so many families moving together, it was more practical for us to move as much as possible on one big boat than to line up extra wagons, oxen, and drivers to take it across land. They hope to reach the Westport, Missouri landing about the time the overland caravan reaches that area.

I'm staying at Bridge's house with their two children this summer. After the group gets settled in Kansas, Bridge and Elizabeth will come back here to get the rest of us moved. Asa went along to look the territory over, so I don't know yet if his family will move or not.

Lucy Curless and the rest of her children will make the trip with us this fall after they get their land sold. This area is filled up with people just like Ohio, with no cheap land for her sons either. I imagine this part of Illinois has changed drastically since you lived here briefly fifteen years ago. I must say I'm happy Lucy has decided to move. That way I won't be the only "old widow" on the trip!

In the meantime, I've started a big garden by Bridge's house with hopes of growing as much produce as possible to take with us. So far this spring Kansas has had a dry spell that has people worried. I loaded most of our belongings on the boat so I can fill my overland wagon with potatoes, dried fruit, and vegetables.

Salina and I will pass our evenings piecing baby quilts. Mary, Nettie, Louise, and Elizabeth are all with child as they travel. We thought it would be a nice surprise to present each new member of our family with a warm quilt this fall. I pulled my sack of material scraps out of a trunk before it was loaded onto the boat. I haven't decided what quilt patterns I will use yet. They should be about moving, don't you think?

Quilting while we wait,

Margaret

Saturday, September 1, 1855
Bluff City, Illinois

Dear Phoebe,

Thought I'd write before we leave for Kansas. We've been waiting for Elizabeth to deliver. She gave birth to Oscar Curless Kennedy on Monday, so we'll leave as soon as she feels strong enough to travel. I'm anxious to get on the trail and rejoin our families in Kansas.

The first group arrived safely in the new territory without any major difficulty. Muddy roads and balky cattle made a slow start, but both got better along the way. I'm sure the girls who made the overland trip will have a different story than Elizabeth's, for she was on the boat. Walking, keeping track of little children, and cooking on a campfire would be different than riding the boat with no children along to worry about.

At the end of the month the wagons ferried across the Missouri River and camped overnight near the bank. While everyone was eating breakfast the next morning, their boat floated by them! They docked at Kansas City and unloaded our cargo onto extra wagons.

Their departure was delayed the next morning by a throng of Wyandot Indians calling on their camp. The women made flapjacks for the hungry group while the Indians challenged the men to wrestling and horse racing. Though this was their initial encounter with the red men, there have been many more meetings now that our family has settled close to the Shawnee reservation that lies in the eastern border of the Kansas Territory. So far the Indians have tolerated the white people crossing their lands to get to the new settlement. I'm not sure I'd be civil to hundreds of people and wagons going through my land.

Bridge made a remark that we didn't have to worry about the Indians as much as the Missourians, but he wouldn't elaborate when I asked what he meant. I hope it does not mean trouble.

On June 2 they stopped on a bluff overlooking the spot the trio had picked out last year. Spring rains had broken the drought, and the Wakarusa River Valley was a deep green wave of grass. Everyone was happy with the scouts' choice of land. When we

18

last heard, they were camping in tents along the river, building cabins, and plowing up native prairie on their claims. Sounds like they have gotten extra work plowing for others in the area, also.

Nettie ended up having Augusta Jane on the trail near the Missouri-Kansas border on the 25th of May. While camped a few days for Nettie's recovery, a horse and cow wandered off, but Scott and Leander went back in July and found them.

They celebrated the Fourth of July by going north into the new town of Lawrence. Remember that red and white skirt I had made for Nettie's little Catherine? They tacked it on a pole and used it as their flag as they drove their wagons into town. They combined food with new Lawrence residents, heard speeches, and felt welcomed into the community.

Got a letter from Nettie that cholera had flared up and then back down again around Fort Riley this summer. The new town of Pawnee, located near the fort, lost its opportunity to be the territorial capital because of the epidemic. She said not to worry because this new fort is a four day ride west of them, but I know the disease had to travel from Missouri to the fort to get there. I know I sound worried, but I'm glad one group got through and that we are waiting until now to cross the prairie.

The next time you hear from me, I'll have traveled across another state and will be settled in my new farm. I'll write you the details of both.

Ready to journey to my new valley home,

Margaret

Tuesday, October 23, 1855
Douglas County, Kansas Territory

Dear Phoebe,

I send you greetings from the territory of Kansas. I'm glad to have that trying journey behind us. Besides us and Bridge's family, Lucy Curless and her six, and the Joseph Shields family of twelve were my companions. My daughter-in-law Mary's brother, John Jones, came along to help with the wagons.

Our wagons were packed tight and heavy, but we still ended up leaving things behind that I had planned to take along. I made the mistake of keeping Hugh's walnut table with me rather than sending it on the boat. I ended up using the top as the lid on the smoked pork barrel to justify its space in the wagon. Now I fear the table will always have a slight smell of cured meat to it.

We brought part of the garden produce I labored to grow this summer and sold the rest. I still think we should have made room or added another wagon and team to bring the food. Maybe I just felt uneasy without my usual cellar full of preserves, but Bridge insisted that the group in Kansas would have grown enough to last the winter. He'll be eating only words this January if he was wrong and his mother was right!

Each night we camped near a water stream or farmhouse for our animals' thirst and our needs. Locating water and firewood, unpacking utensils from the wagon, preparing and cooking the meal took a good share of our evenings.

The boys hunted wild game to save on our supplies. Stewed possum reminded me of my childhood when my brothers supplemented our family's meals with their trapping along the river.

I never thought of it before this trip, but coffee has a distinct flavor when it's made with river water. It is not a taste I relished, only tolerated for want of something hot to drink after a long day. I quickly learned to fill a jug of water whenever we came across a well and tuck it in the wagon so we could have clean cup of coffee the next time we stopped for a meal.

Trying to bake decent bread over a campfire become Lucy's obsession. Seems like there was always a crusty layer of dirt and ashes crowning the loaf. Her boys teased her one night that she was using dried manure for flavoring to save on the spices. They went three nights without bread for that remark. Lucy held her umbrella over the campfire more than once to shield the flames and her open skillet from the rain and wind.

On Saturday nights we tried to set up camp in time to wash clothes. That gave the garments all day Sunday to dry before they were packed back in the wagon. Even though it is supposed to be a day of rest Sunday, we spent those afternoons and evenings preparing food for the next few days on the trail.

We slept under the stars and among the mosquitoes. I whip-stitched two old quilts, the Indian Trails and the Log Cabin, together at the top and we threw them over a ridge pole to use as a tent. My Dolly Madison's Star quilt was used as bedding one cool night and got ruined in the mud. I was glad I shipped my good quilts ahead on the boat. The dust on the trail and the mud in the wash water was hard on our clothing and bedding.

The weather cooperated most of the time. Because it was September we had bearable temperatures, except for a few chilly nights. We hit a patch of fog near the river at Quincy, Illinois, and four days of rain and mud crossing eastern Missouri.

Getting used to walking ten to fifteen miles a day put a few blisters on our heels, but we got used to it after the first week. We sometimes rode in the wagon for a rest, but it added weight for the oxen to pull, so I usually walked alongside the animals instead. Elizabeth's newborn probably rode the best, sleeping away in his basket while the wagon rocked him.

Red mud sticking to our shoes and hems was another nuisance. I'm still washing the Missouri dirt off everything, from clothing to pots and pans.

Our main problem was the attitude of the people we met along the way. We had no problems traveling over the Illinois prairie, but after crossing the Mississippi River at Quincy, things changed. Our passage through Missouri was a lesson in keeping a quiet and civil tongue. The Missourians immediately questioned our state's origin to find out if we were for or against slavery. At first I spoke up about my beliefs that all men should be free but soon found out water would be denied to us at farmsteads because of my words. Bridge became our spokesman and the rest of us stayed in camp rather than mingle with the farm families. It would have been pleasant to visit with the women, but our "notions" against their beliefs would have gotten us in trouble.

We were even asked if we were Mormons for we had so many women and so few men in our group. Joseph Shields was not amused at being accused of being a bigamist. The four extra adult women in his group were his daughters, not wives. So many Mormons from Naveroo, Illinois, have crossed the state on their way west that people have become suspicious of them and their strange ways.

The men started milking the cows, much to both their and the cows' chagrin, because if we women milked, it gave us away as Northerners. But that helped spell us for the cooking and daily chores.

The Southern attitude affected our weekly worship also. The first Sunday we camped near an Illinois town and enjoyed the local church service. We had to abandon our Sunday ritual in Missouri because we were not welcome.

We were glad to get to the Missouri River, where we crossed at Randolph's Ferry. Three days later we were overlooking our new valley home.

Yellow and orange hues were starting to touch the deep green landscape of the valley when we arrived. In the distance we could follow the ribbon of timber that hugs the bank of the Wakarusa River. Tiny patches of newly turned fields and maturing corn formed a patchwork in the native grass. Sounds of people industriously working their new claims drifted up to us. I wish I could have seen it two years ago, before the land was turned. Progress is changing the landscape daily.

Our caravan wound down the hill to the valley floor below to the land that Bridge claimed for us in June. We're on flat river bottom land, with no trees in the way to clear for the fields. I was startled at first by the starkness, but now I like to look out over the waving grass to the bluffs in the distance.

I questioned my dwelling when we stopped on my land. I think this one-room timber shack could blow over in a stiff breeze. Tom apologized, saying they needed to raise a quick house on each claim to make the properties looked lived on to ward off claim jumpers. Since they have been busy plowing fields, the boys haven't started building us a regular house yet.

This will be our temporary home for the winter, and we'll start building next spring. This way it will give us time to pick the right spot for the house in respect to the farm.

My first home is a combination of rough-cut timber and split shakes, with a bare minimum of chinking. I can see through the walls in more than one place.

Unfortunately, gaps in the walls means it is very easy for small creatures to come and go as they please. I've found nests of mice in every possible place. All food must be kept sealed in earthen jars or tins.

The boys told us about the numerous encounters they have had with rattlesnakes in the prairie grass. I assumed I would be spared that pleasure, for it was autumn now, but I was wrong. One morning a rattler came out from under our bed, slithering across the floor, heading for a spot by the warmth of the fireplace.

I plan to do some improvements on the walls myself for obvious reasons.

There is only one room, about a quarter the size of my whole Ohio house, and it is going to be crowded for four of us. (I hung up the photograph I had taken of me and the girls in front of our Ohio home, to remind me that we will eventually have a solid house again!)

By the time we set up two beds, a table of split boards, and two crude benches made of split logs, our house was full. We stacked packing crates against one wall to store our household supplies. Clothes are still in trunks because I have no wardrobe closet yet.

We filled the mattress ticking with prairie hay, which seems to be matting down already and harboring bugs, and piled the bedding on top. Extra quilts will stay in the trunk until cold weather comes.

Would you believe there was a rocking chair waiting for me beside the fireplace?! Bridge picked one up for me on their boat trip, for he knew I'd miss my rocker in Ohio. My thoughtful children wanted to ease the transition for me. Quarters are so close in this house, I'll have to watch so I don't set my dress on fire while I'm sitting in it!

The biggest surprise on my new land was a spindly apple sapling in front of the house. The boys wanted to make me feel at home, so they bought one in Westport and planted it when they picked out my land. It will be a long time before there is a branch strong enough to hold a swing, but I intend to be here to see my grandchildren use it.

No barn, granary, or chicken house has been erected yet. A split-rail fence is the only protection for the animals. After I got here, Tom built a little lean-to against the house for the chickens I brought along on the trail.

Joe and Mary's and Cate and Collins' claims lie to the south of us. Bridge chose ground bordering the river three miles northeast of us. All the Curless families are near to hand.

Scott and Louise's land is directly east of me. They talked about putting one dwelling on the property line between our two places for both families, but with so many claim jumpers in the area, they decided to build two.

Luckily the one well they dug between us is close to my house. Mary wants a well before winter strikes so she doesn't have to walk to my place in the snow for a bucket of water.

Scott built a dugout for their first home. This type of earth shelter is supposed to be warmer in the winter and cooler during the summer. We saw several on our way through Missouri. The sod in the space where the house will be is broken with a plow. The sod is cut with a shovel into rectangle shapes resembling large bricks. A hole, four to eight feet deep, is dug out where the sod has been removed. The sod bricks are laid around the outer edge of the hole for support walls, then timber and sod are layered for the roof. For people with nothing else to use, this is the most practical home to build on the prairie.

Scott plans to plaster the inside walls with sand and clay and whitewash them to seal the interior and make it brighter. He is waiting to to this because the roof has not set and sealed well yet. Every time it rains, it drips inside for days.

Their worst problem so far have been vermin burrowing into their roof and falling down inside once they go through the ceiling. I was sitting on a bench there the first day, and I felt a dusting of dirt falling in my hair. Looking up, I saw a pair of beady eyes staring back at me.

Bridge built a log cabin on his claim last summer when they scouted the area. He thought we would be moving right away. Because it's on the river, Bridge used walnut and oak cut from the banks. It was built on a sled, for he didn't know exactly where the land boundaries were at the time. His forethought means that his land in the only one bordering the river. He was prepared when he had to move it this fall. With the help of men and oxen, the house was pulled to its new location. Baby Oscar slept inside, snug in his log cradle, while the cabin was moved.

So far I haven't had much time to meet neighbors outside our Kennedy Valley. When I was over to Bridge's yesterday, I met the John Pieratt family, who helped with the move. John and his wife, Deborah, have seven children, ages fourteen to a new boy born in August. I started to clam up out of habit when I heard her Southern drawl, but Elizabeth explained that this was the family Bridge met last year when they were scouting for land. Even though they are Southerners, they don't believe in slavery. Deborah was congenial and happy to see more women moving into the area. It didn't take me long to relax my guard around her. Her description of their first winter here will help me prepare my household for the months ahead.

I'm glad Salina will have other young people in the area to socialize with. Melvina Curless is the only one of our valley that is near her age. Salina's siblings are much older than she, and the nieces and nephews are all under six years of age.

There is an abrupt hill to the east of the Pieratt's land called Blue Mound. It has a mysterious gray haze to it almost any time of day you look at it. The Pieratt children promised Salina an exploration trip to its top when we come over to visit.

Sunday we explored the two new towns growing near us. They are totally opposite of civilized Hamersville, Ohio, with its brick buildings, streets, and sidewalks that I took for granted.

Lawrence, six miles to the north of us, has a hotel made out of loose hay staked against poles! Buildings are being built as rapidly as possible, but most businesses are selling merchandise out of tents. There are few women in town so far and no church in sight. The majority of the people are from Boston. Their move was sponsored by the Emigrant Aid Society. Lawrence is definitely a free-state town.

Franklin, on the other hand, is the congregating place for proslavers. Southern gentlemen seem rowdy away from their plantations. They also left their women at home Down South because I didn't see any walking around town. Franklin is about the same distance from us as Lawrence, only to the northeast. Its building situation is the same as Lawrence's.

Houses in both towns are slow being built because there are not enough sawmills to fill the demand for lumber. Please tell Maggie that her brother, William James, arrived safely and is working in a new sawmill in Lawrence.

I wish you could see it, Phoebe. It is so different from Ohio's old established farmsteads, orchards, stone fences, and carefully tended fields. People here are living in tents or hasty shacks, trying to raise some kind of shelter before winter sets in. The wildness here is so primitive and dangerous, but so exciting, too.

Hugh would have loved the challenge of taming the prairie. He has been in my thoughts so much this last year as we planned and carried out this trip. I hated to leave his grave, but I'm glad I journeyed to Kansas to see our children carry out their dreams.

This letter, though long, only tells a portion of what I've experienced these past months. You know me well enough to read between the lines and to know what ups and downs I've been through. It has been quite a journey in more ways than one, and I'm glad it is over.

Settling in my new little shack,

Margaret

Friday, December 21, 1855
Douglas County, Kansas Territory

Dear Phoebe,

Season's blessings to you and your family. Please pass on my Christmas greeting to my old neighbors and friends.

In many ways I wish that I and my family were back in Ohio this Christmas. At times I get homesick thinking of the church festivities and neighborhood gatherings I'm missing this month. And so much has happened since we arrived that life is very discouraging, and I'm afraid dangerous at times.

Your last letter commented on what you have heard about the problems here in the territory. I'm afraid the news you get in your newspapers tells only a little of the actual affliction it is causing the people.

Slavery and abolition is tearing this territory apart. I can't believe how grown civilized men can fight each other about a righteous cause that is so clear. It is not safe to travel at all. Men are being shot in cold blood just down the road from here.

I worry constantly about my sons. I taught them to stand up for what is right, but they shouldn't have to carry a gun to protect themselves while out in their own fields. Neighborhood men have formed groups to protect their families against the roving proslavers who are causing the major problems. It is very disheartening for my daughters and daughters-in-law to see their husbands walk out the door and wonder if they'll be back. I worry how much bloodshed will happen before this state is formed.

Tension mounts every time there is an election. Thousands of armed Missourians have crossed the border, raiding the voting stations and stuffing the ballot boxes for slavery. They are not territory residents, but the government still recognized the elections as the legal vote of the people. Now it is illegal for us to speak out against slavery, with the threat of jail or death if we disobey.

The Free State Party hosted a convention in Topeka this fall and drew up its own constitution prohibiting slavery, but it is not being recognized by the territorial governor or the United States Congress. It does not help that the latest governor, Wilson Shannon, sided with the Missourians, ignoring the problems until they escalated this month. It pains me that he was Ohio's governor for two terms in the '40s and has turned his back on the free-staters.

And the sad reality is that there are very few slaves in the territory—and never will be—because most of the land has been settled by Northerners. Why must Missouri force their choice of life on us?

Last month the county exploded when Franklin Coleman, a proslaver, shot free-stater Charles Dow in a quarrel about their boundary line down by Hickory Point. Coleman, along with his neighbor, Mr. Buckley, fled to the Shawnee Methodist Mission, the proslavery capital, and he turned himself over to the Douglas County Sheriff (who is a proslaver living in Westport, Missouri). Free-staters met at Jacob Branson's, who had witnessed the murder, and decided they needed to seek their own justice, for the law won't do it. Then someone burned down Coleman's and Buckley's cabins, causing Buckley to ask Sheriff Jones to arrest Branson. The sheriff and his posse arrested Branson during the night and headed back north through the county.

Someone found out about the warrant and alerted the neighborhood men to gather at the Abbotts' house, just two miles east of me, to plan a rescue of Branson. A neighbor stopped here to get Tom and Leander, but they were out on an expedition of their own. Joe and Mary took the children out of bed, wrapped them in quilts, and ran them over to the Holloways' house. Collins took off with Joe and Will and Edmond Curless, leaving the wives together to protect the children.

Abbott's house is right along the road that the posse would pass by. A group of fifteen men stopped Jones and his group as they rode by the house and freed Branson after a verbal confrontation. Jones vowed to retaliate against Lawrence for their intervention. (Joe said Mrs. Abbott was the calmest of the group, getting everyone's guns ready before they confronted the posse. He thinks she also had a gun pointed out the west window, ready to help if gunfire broke out.)

Sheriff Jones went to Franklin and planned his revenge against the free-staters. He wrote to Governor Shannon, asking for aid to put down an "open rebellion." The Governor didn't investigate the problem, but ordered the Kansas Militia to ready themselves, and sent word to President Pierce that he needed federal soldiers from Fort Leavenworth to attack Lawrence.

Meanwhile, Jones rounded up Missouri men and disgruntled Indians, promising they could rid the country of the free-state headquarters. During the week fifteen hundred camped south of Franklin waiting for the command from Shannon. Those border ruffians harassed innocent travelers, stealing their goods and detaining them.

Around eight hundred free-state men from all over the area convened to help defend Lawrence. Some of the larger settlements sent companies of men. They built earthen log barricades on the streets that lead into town, distributed Sharps rifles, and drilled for the confrontations. Alarmed at the rising situation, two men from Lawrence slipped through the proslavery lines to explain their side of the story to Shannon.

Shannon finally came to Lawrence and settled the "Wakarusa War" with an uneasy treaty between the two sides. Fortunately, the Missourians were cold and out of whiskey, so they were ready to go home. I fear the peace will not last. And my sons are still on Jones' list of problem free-staters he wants to arrest.

We women have had to gather firewood from the river timber this month because the men have been gone or are in hiding. We leave all the children in care of a few mothers and head for the Wakarusa with the wagon and oxen. So far, women have not been detained or molested in this war between sides.

I've taught Salina how to shoot a gun. There was never the need for girls to learn how to shoot in Ohio. It is against our Christian belief to show a person how to take deadly aim against a fellow man, but my motherly instincts told me she has to know how to protect herself if she has no choice.

I've tried to help neighboring families, especially the children, during all this. Fears for their family, especially when their fathers are gone so much, make it very hard on them. This fall I taught school for a few weeks before the war broke out. Many children used to go to school before they moved to the territory. They need to learn their letters and their sums, even in this savage place.

Since we do not have a schoolhouse, we met in Scott's dugout, which was the warmest place to meet. I kept the children all day. They brought beans, firewood, or whatever they could manage, and I'd make a big pot of soup for our noon meal. In the dim light we'd recite stories, poems, multiplication numbers, sing songs, anything we could think of to keep occupied without the use of books, slates, or paper.

Most of the children were from Northern states, but I had one little girl who educated us all to the ways and songs of the South. One of the children's favorite songs to sing was a lullaby this girl's black mammy used to sing to her at bedtime. These children from different backgrounds can get along together. Why can't their fathers?

We did get old issues of the *Herald of Freedom*, the Lawrence newspaper, to read. The copies were so worn after being passed around the neighborhood that the children couldn't read the articles where the paper folded, but at least we could study the words and letters.

It pains me to think of all the books I left behind in Ohio that are so desperately needed now. If you can round up any books and send them to me when the trouble here calms down, I would surely appreciate it. We need to help the children who are caught in this war, or there won't be another generation to carry on the free-state cause.

As the weather turns colder, so does this house. It seems so much colder here than in Ohio, probably because there is nothing to stop the blasts of frigid air that sweep the barren plains.

Our candle supply is nearly gone. For light we're burning a braided rag wick set in a pie plate of wild animal fat, saved from the boys' hunts for food. The flicker of the light is never still, often blowing out when the cabin door opens.

Our first blizzard lasted days, piling snow up against the house to the rooftop. The dwelling was the only thing to catch the snow as it flew across the prairie. Snowflakes whistle by here horizontally like they were shot from a cannon.

The grass and mud I chunked between the timber of the walls keeps out the worst wind, but not the cold. I've plastered the newspapers we had to the walls, but you can watch the paper move where air blows between the spaces. Some mornings there has been a fine layer of unmelted snow covering us and our beds against the wall. The ice is so thick on the outside—and inside—of our only window that we can't see out.

Food turns cold very quickly away from the fireplace. The water bucket has a layer of ice on top by morning. My earthen jar of yeast that I brought all the way from Ohio chilled and died.

I worry about frostbite with the frigid temperatures this week. We don't have any spare gunpowder or lard to mix into a salve to ease the pain. I'm rarely without my cloak on inside or outside the house because it has been so cruelly cold. Salina and I have worn three layers of underdrawers and socks all month. Leggings made of animal skins, with the hair side inward, has saved our legs from total misery.

I'm worried that we might run out of food before the winter is over. Some of us women are often too worried to eat, but we need fuel in our bodies to fight the cold. They didn't get much in the way of garden produce grown here when they arrived in June. Sod corn and hay is the main supply of food we have for ourselves and the livestock.

Between the weather and the border ruffians' raids, supplies coming into the state have been unpredictable. As I watch our food vanish, I think of the cellar full of preserved food I had in Ohio. As I write this, my mouth waters for a bowl of preserved peaches and a slice of Christmas fruitcake.

Mary and Louise delivered baby girls, so there is extra stress and concern for them. With four babies under a year old, I worry about their survival this winter. I've spent several nights at my children's homes doctoring sick grandchildren with what little medicine I brought along. I used up my supply of mustard for chest plasters. So many times I have thought of Hamersville's pharmacy and our old family doctor.

Please tell Maggie that her brother was out recently to see me. For your information only—William James had to change jobs because the sawmill he was working at blew up. Fortunately he was not there at the time, because a worker was killed in the blast. He has been heavily involved in the free-state issue also, so add him to your prayers.

So far I am holding up as best I can. I need to stay strong to hold my family together. I am their mother, and it is up to me to sustain my children's faith and keep them alive in this bitter territory.

Praying for relief from our misery,

Margaret

Bleeding Kansas

Sunday, February 24, 1856
Douglas County, Kansas Territory

Dear Phoebe,

I apologize for not writing this winter. Between the weather and the border problems, survival has taken all our strength these past months. Mail has not gone out with any regularity, so I hope this letter eventually reaches you.

We've had over eight weeks of extreme cold. The cold is just starting to release its hold on the country. I won't say a cross word about summer heat if it ever gets here. I was beginning to fear I'd be found frozen stiff in bed one morning until Tom bought a buffalo hide to add to the bedding. I whipstitched strips of cloth on the corners of my quilts and hung them on hooks nailed to the walls to add a layer of insulation to the shack during the day.

We moved into Scott's dugout during the worst of the cold because we were getting frostbite in our drafty home. It was so cold that spending any time outside shelter was dangerous. The newspaper reported it got down to thirty below zero on Christmas day. If we didn't get up during the night to put more wood on the hearth fire, it would be stone cold by morning. If it went out, one of us would have to go to another's farm to get live coals to renew our heat source because we have no more matches.

And we have run out of food. Coffee and flour were depleted by the middle of January. Even if we could have gotten into town, store supplies dwindled to nothing because shipments from the East were stopped by impassable roads. We've lived on corn this last month, eating it in every possible form, from corn bread to hominy.

The livestock that we herded from Illinois are thin from hunger. New calves have found warmth near my home hearth more than once. Some didn't make it through the winter. It has been too cold for the hens to lay eggs. Some chickens ended up in the stewpot. They would have frozen to death if we hadn't eaten them.

Indians have been in the same situation. I don't know how they kept warm and fed in this miserable weather. More than once one man or band of Indians have walked into my home, asking for food.

A neighbor had an unusual experience with the Indians. She was making lye soap in a kettle outside the house, and a trio came up to the fire. The mixture of lye water boiling together with animal fat must have smelled like food to the hungry Indians. They thought she didn't want to share when the woman shook her head "no," so they seized the spoon and took a bit of the thickening soap. Tears came to their eyes, but each tasted the mixture before they left.

At least the neighborhood confrontations were minimal during the cold weather. Now as the weather warms up, the skirmishes begin again. Fanatics on both sides are shooting people, giving the territory its deserved name, Bleeding Kansas.

Last week I panicked when I went out at dawn and saw large bootprints in the fresh snow around the house. Someone had been prowling our claim during the night. We're not safe in our own homes.

The Free State Party had another election on January 15th. Missourians tried to interfere, especially in Leavenworth County, before the election by sending written notices to settlers in hopes of scaring them out of the territory. Companies of free-staters guarded the polls on Election Day and drove the ruffians out. Dr. Robinson from Lawrence was voted in as Governor, but Congress denounced its legislature and the men involved, so now the party is in defiance of the law. The ruffians have declared open war against the free-staters again.

The males in our family are back in hiding. Sheriff Jones is still trying to arrest the men who rescued Branson from him. The boys have dug a series of holes along the riverbank, lined with hides and covered with brush, that they can burrow into. I don't know how long this can go on before one of my family is seriously hurt or killed.

Now that we've survived the winter, will we survive the war? I hope my next letter to you has news of relief, in both areas.

Cold, tired, but alive,

Margaret

Wednesday, May 28, 1856
Douglas County, Kansas Territory

Dear Phoebe,

The war between the two factions has hit home. Mary's brother, John Jones, was killed on the 18th of this month. Three Southerners stopped at the store at Blanton's Bridge looking for Blanton. The store owner saw them coming and hid, leaving John and another young man in the shack. The men harassed John, but told him he could leave if he left his gun behind. John did so, loaded up the sack of flour he had come for, and headed to his claim that is a mile and a half south of the bridge. Before John got two rods from the store, one of the men shot him in the back. Mrs. Blanton dragged John into her house to try to save him. Bridge heard the shot, for he lives next to Blanton, and ran over to help. Unfortunately, John died that night. He was buried in an unmarked grave on Blue Mound.

John Jones helped us move last fall. During the winter he went back to Illinois to get his mother and other sister. Mrs. Jones and her daughter moved in with Joe and Mary for the time being. They haven't decided whether to stay on John's claim or sell it and move back to Illinois. Mrs. Jones and I talked at length the other night. The cold murder of her son has devastated her and she needed the strong shoulder of a friend. What can we mothers do to protect our children in situations like this?

When there's a knock on the door in the middle of the night, I don't know if it's one of my boys needing food or a border ruffian looking for them instead. Tom and Leander are gone days at a time, either hiding or patrolling Lawrence or another free-state town. When they do come home up, they are so exhausted that I stand guard while they sleep.

One night Leander sneaked in carrying a new Sharps rifle. When I asked him where he got it, Leander said he was carrying a "Beecher Bible," compliments of a Pastor Beecher and his congregation in New England. Groups from Back East have been sending firearms in boxes marked books and Bibles so they can get them through to the free-staters.

Phoebe, this is not what I anticipated when we decided to move to Kansas. My family should be cultivating our homesteads, not hiding in the timber, holding a gun bead on every stranger that passes by. Meanwhile, the men are tortured with anxiety and guilt, for their young wives and children are home alone to contend with the threats of murder and arson.

I loathe the anger that is building up in my heart. It is unchristian to hate your fellow man, but I quit praying to save ruffians' souls after I saw my neighbor's husband murdered and her home burned. How can someone do that to another soul? How would the ruffians feel if these were their families being threatened? Is that what they are afraid of, that we will raid Missouri and ravage their families and farms if they don't get rid of us first?

The other night ruffians came looking for Lafayette over at Lucy's house. They searched the place from top to bottom. When they looked under her bed, she had enough. Lucy grabbed the tea kettle full of boiling water and threatened to scald their eyes out. She was lucky they left the house standing around her.

There's a point when your patience gets thin and you are no longer afraid. Many women have gotten to that stage. Crops should have been planted and up by now, but that's not the case this spring. The men are out fighting, leaving the women to do everything from trying to plow and sow seed—if they dare venture outside—to taking care of children and livestock, if the latter hasn't already been taken. All the while being harassed and having things filched by the marauders.

I planted a garden, but as soon as the lettuce was up it was stolen out of the ground! I fear the rest of my produce will end up in the stomachs of the ruffians going by, not in my needy family's. It doesn't help to keep a gun handy either. Southern men are gentlemanly to women unless they are armed, then females are the enemy just the same as a free-state man.

Tension is high among the neighbors because there are so many different opinions on the situation. Several are not really on either side: they don't believe in slavery, but they don't want Negroes living in the community, so they halfheartedly favor the proslavers. I know of two families that have been picked on by both sides.

No homestead is totally safe from intrusion. Anyone going by a claim can tell if the family is from the North or the South by the construction of the house. Different regions of the country make their joint corners differently.

Some neighbors are doing better by staying neutral, like as the Pieratts. Being from the South, they seem to have been overlooked by the ruffians ransacking homesteads. Deborah has been wondering if some of her family who took claims in Cass County, Missouri, are part of the ruffian groups. She searches every face in the groups that go by her house, wondering if a family member is riding along. She hasn't gotten a letter from her sister-in-law in months.

Sheriff Jones is at it again. In April he tried to make an arrest in Lawrence, but citizens just "happened" to help the person escape. The next week someone shot the sheriff, but he recovered. Lawrence denounced the act, saying free-staters had no part in the attack, but warrants for charges of treason were issued for the town leaders: Robinson, Lane, and others. The newspapers were indicted for printing antislavery information.

Border ruffians convened to the Wakarusa River again, preparing to attack Lawrence. It was one of these groups that killed John Jones.

On the 21st, about eight hundred ruffians with Sheriff Jones and former senator Atchison from Missouri invaded the town. Lawrence citizens offered no resistance so as not to make matters worse. The presses in the *Herald of Freedom* and the *Kansas Free State* newspaper offices were destroyed and the metal type dumped into the river. A cannon, nicknamed Old Sacramento because it was first used in the Mexican War, was set up in front of the newly opened Free State Hotel, with the drunk Atchison firing the first shot. The hotel was blasted and burned and town stores were looted. On the way out they set fire to Governor Robinson's house.

A few days later John Brown, who lives near Osawatomie, and some of his sons brutally hacked to death some proslavers down on Pottawatomie Creek. People believe these murders were in retaliation for the latest attack on Lawrence. I don't condone the man and his action, but maybe it will help the proslavers realize we are not going to take their murdering and rampaging anymore.

Right now the Missouri River and overland routes through Missouri are cut off to free-state traffic. Settlers are being turned back and emigrant aid is being seized as contraband by the proslavers. Men from Southern states, without their families, are coming to Kansas, not to settle land, but to help the Missourians "uphold the honor and rights of the South." Federal troops have been called out to help the proslavery side, so I fear there is going to be a major confrontation soon.

Deborah is mailing this letter for me through the Franklin post office so it will go through. For now, please send your letters to me in an envelope addressed to: Deborah Pieratt, Franklin, Kansas Territory.

I'm sure you realize these letters to you are my way to vent my angers and fears. I need you, dear friend, but I am truly thankful that you are not here to witness the trouble. Thank you for your letters. Even though you are miles away, you are still my shoulder of support.

With anger and despair,

Margaret

Sunday, November 2, 1856
Douglas County, Kansas Territory

Dear Phoebe,

I just received your letter addressed September 10. I am finally able to assure you that we have survived the terrible ordeal of this summer. You mentioned other letters that you and Sarah wrote, but due to the situation at the border this summer, I'm sure your letters were burned in a ruffian's campfire before they got to Douglas County. I know you and my family have been frantic with worry over our situation. The tension escalated to an all-out war by the end of May.

After Brown murdered those men in May, things changed for the worst. The Southerners were caught off-guard when the free-state people started fighting back. Up to then, the proslavers could harass people and the free-staters kept themselves in check to prevent more bodily harm and property damage. More recruited groups from the South were organized to drive all the free-staters out for the last time. Bands of men stole through the countryside, plundering homesteaders along their path. Many homesteaders on both sides fled the territory if they could.

We debated whether to combine our households to protect the children, or stay apart so we wouldn't all be together in the worst situation. Should the house look abandoned so the ruffians don't stop, or will they spend the night in our beds, ransacking and burning the houses anyway? We ended up mixing some of the households, but we kept hearth fires burning in all of the houses when possible.

Bridge brought Elizabeth and their children over to get them away from potential trouble. They were too close to the Blanton Bridge, which the ruffians use to cross the Wakarusa.

Salina has spent most of her time trying to help keep thirteen children occupied, for we don't dare let them wander outside. Cate delivered another child, Emery, during all this.

Most of the time I stayed on my homestead, trying to protect the milk cow and horses I had tied to the back of the house. Our other animals were gone, but I wanted to keep the cow so we could have milk for the children. More than once I led old Bossy in the house for safekeeping.

I figured I had the most chance, acting like a frail old lady, to win that situation. Little did the ruffians know I had a little derringer in my hand, tucked into the folds of my skirt, whenever they went by. My standing guard, though, did not keep the ruffians from coming up into the yard and snatching chickens on the run to cook over their campfires.

I buried my valuables and our money outside, away from the house. Money didn't do us any good, for there was no food to buy even if we could have gotten to Lawrence. With the continued situation of supplies being cut off at the border, things got hopeless in the country. There were nearly two thousand people desperate for food because we couldn't even get a sack of flour through the lines. What could we do but fight back to save our families?

The first confrontation on June 2 the Battle of Black Jack, near Prairie City, happened as free-staters faced Captain Pate. He had raided Palmyra and captured several free-staters while out looking for John Brown. After a battle of gunfire, our group— John Brown, Leander, and Will included—captured the proslavers and recovered stolen property. A few days later they exchanged their prisoners for free-state men that were being held by the territorial militia.

The proslavers started stockpiling provisions and ammunition in four places around the country, mostly supplies intended for or stolen from the settlers.

James Lane, who had traveled Back East to recruit help, led settlers to the territory through Iowa and Nebraska in the first part of August. Finding out the dire situation of the free-state people, Lane organized an army to attack the proslavery strongholds. The proslavers immediately fled the Osawatomie fort when Lane's army attacked it on the 5th of August.

Fort Franklin proved harder to crack on the 12th. A small group tried to take the fort in June, but achieved nothing more than raiding a proslavery store and taking some food and ammunition. This time they pushed a wagon full of burning hay up against the building, causing the occupants to surrender. William

James was the first to enter and disarm the captain in charge of the fort. They recaptured the cannon, Old Sacramento that had been taken from Lawrence in May. It was standing up in the corner of the building, dressed in a gown and veil!

Over four hundred free-staters descended onto Fort Saunders next. Upon seeing so many ready to attack, the men in the fort fled.

The cannon was set up in front of Fort Titus on the 16th. Cannonballs had been made from melted-down type salvaged from the destruction of the newspaper offices. On the first shot everyone yelled, "Here comes the new issue of the *Herald of Freedom*!" After the sixth shot, the fort raised the white flag of surrender.

The government called upon the militia to stamp out the free-staters. Soldiers and Missourians burned down Osawatomie, then clashed with groups of free-staters in that area the whole last week of August. Those proslavers were driven back to Missouri.

Government officials, including Governor Shannon, fled the territory, fearing free-staters would attack Lecompton next.

While the free-state guards were in the southern part of the state, more raids and arrests on our people were made around Lawrence. When Lane's army came back, they marched on to Lecompton and freed those prisoners.

The territory was given a third governor, John Geary, but the proslavery territorial officials disregarded his orders, recruiting twenty-seven hundred ruffians to surround Lawrence in the middle of September. Governor Geary arrived just in time with U.S. troops to back him against the ruffians. He ordered the commanders of the proslavery groups to disband and leave immediately. They left the territory but plundered their way back to Missouri.

Currently we can travel along the roads that were once the paths of murdering ruffians. Things almost seem back to normal, until we pass a neighbor's cabin with just the blacked chimney stones left standing. The countryside looks like a battleground, not a promising community.

The men from our neighborhood were gone from our homesteads almost the entire summer. Frequently we'd hear reports of what was going on around the country, but we had no idea if they were safe. The worry and constant danger almost drove people insane. I can't describe the relief I felt when all my boys straggled home.

They came back changed men, though, with horrors of bloody confrontations reflected in their eyes. They used to listen with revered attention to how their ancestors bravely fought at Valley Forge during the Revolution. They thought it would be glorious to be soldiers and win the battles. Now they realize that the old veterans left out the grisly truth of war in their stories.

All were in need of decent food and uninterrupted sleep. For the first week back, Leander's nightmares were so bad at times that I could not wake him out of his terrifying trance. Time is slowly healing some of the memories of things my youngest son saw, but I'm sure others will haunt him forever. I hope my sons never have to defend their beliefs and their land with violence again.

Tom came driving in with a wagon of provisions they had confiscated from a ruffian's camp. I was relieved to see both. I felt a slight twinge of guilt using the provisions, not knowing who they were originally intended for, but our families have had so much stolen over the past year, that one wagon of supplies doesn't compensate our losses—and it won't last the winter either.

Last week when I dug into a sack of flour brought home in that wagon, I scooped up a little linen pouch of jewelry. It contained a wedding band, a gold locket, and a cameo brooch. Many women have had their jewelry stolen in the raids that went on this past year. Some had their rings yanked right off their fingers by looters. Apparently a woman hid her valuables in the flour, hoping to keep them safe. Leander suggested we sell them for money, but I refused. We have no idea what part of the territory this loot came from, but I'll try to return the jewelry to its rightful owner, if possible. Being a widow, I know how important the ring is to that wife and what the gesture of its return would mean to me.

We are all back on our individual homesteads, trying to get ready for winter. We never got any improvements done on the houses except throwing a bank of earth and hay against the outside walls. I pray this winter won't be as bad as the last.

Our overrun fences have needed to be rebuilt. Some of our cattle were found, others I'm sure were driven into Missouri or eaten by ruffian armies.

It was impossible to get much of a crop planted or harvested, so we'll have to depend on provisions sent from Northern sympathizers and what we can find on the land. We've combed the riverbanks for wild fruit, herbs, honey, game, anything to help out. Deborah Pieratt suggested we dig dandelion roots to roast and grind for a coffee substitute.

Instead of drinking the buttermilk when I make butter this fall, I am storing it in a barrel to use when the cows go dry this winter. It can be used as a beverage or in cooking. Our house gets cold enough during the winter to keep the buttermilk chilled.

I'm afraid we're in for another hard winter.

The *Herald of Freedom* is back in publication, six months after the press was destroyed and the printer imprisoned. I noticed the new motto on the front page is "Truth Crushed to Earth Shall Rise Again." I hope their prophecy it correct and our problems are over. I pray that peace will finally settle over our valley for good this time.

Leery of winter and our fragile peace,

Margaret

Making Progress

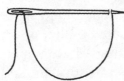

Sunday, April 26, 1857
Douglas County, Kansas Territory

Dear Phoebe,

The cold, cheerless grip of an early spring continues to hold our countryside hostage. Even though I'm wearing my heavy shawl, I don't feel warm today. We've hardly had a hint of sunshine and warmth yet this year. Riding home from church today, I noticed the trees down by the river lacked the tiny new leaves that we saw by the end of last April.

Grass is still dormant in most areas. The little bit of sod wheat I got planted last fall is thick because of good moisture, but it hasn't started its burst of growth.

You can probably tell I'm feeling a little melancholy today because I can't seem to shake the chill of this last winter out of my old bones. I'm needing a good warm soak in bright sunlight to break my mood—as do my chickens.

The four hens that survived the winter, war, and stewpot are late setting eggs. But eventually I'll have a clutch of new chicks to restart my flock. (And all of our mouths are watering for some young fried chicken, before an egg has even hatched!)

I'm anxiously awaiting the burst of spring because it finally holds promise of a good year. One fine week of sunshine will change the whole landscape.

Supplies have been slow coming up the Missouri River because high water has made navigating difficult. A steamboat did get up the Kansas River in early April. It wasn't stopped by weather or border ruffians, so it was a major event, celebrated by the firing of the Old Sacramento.

I made a batch of sugar cookies from the provisions I bought from that boat. They were a belated Christmas treat to my grandchildren. To think I used to make dozens of Christmas cookies in Ohio and never worried about running out of flour and sugar. It had been months since I had either in my cupboard, and I decided to celebrate by baking.

We're finally making progress on our claims. Although it has been too wet to work and plant fields, we've been able to work on other projects. Earlier this year the boys cleared timber down on Bridge's claim to harvest logs for outbuildings. Late winter was the perfect time to do this, while the trees are dormant and free of their leaves. With the ground frozen, the teams could pull across the fields without getting the heavy load stuck in the mud. Working as a team, the boys have been putting up a building on each place.

Yesterday a pile of logs was delivered in my yard. I went out to watch the unloading and Leander jokingly told me that I could take over and erect the shed. I told him it won't be the first building I've constructed in my lifetime!

I hope they cut enough logs for a chicken house also. The thought just crossed my mind to give the chickens my drafty place and start over on the house. Something solid with a raised plank floor instead of packed dirt; a window facing every direction; a front and back door; a separate room for a bedroom. . . . I think you understand my dream.

We've talked about building a new house across the road from this one, because we'll need more homes when the all boys marry. It is exhausting but exhilarating to think of the work we need to do on our land.

It is amazing how fast people are building, or in some cases rebuilding, homesteads and towns. Now that the area situation has calmed down, everyone is trying to make up for lost time.

The government of the new territory is still undecided whether it will become a free or slave state, but at least the open raids have died down. Sheriff Jones resigned his post, so that should help the situation.

We've changed territorial governors again. Geary tried to do justice for the good of the people, but the territorial proslavery legislature was against him. When an attempt was made on his life, Geary sent his resignation to President Buchanan and fled the territory. We'll see if the new governor, Robert Walker, does any better at keeping the peace.

I hear there is still sporadic fighting going on in the southeast part of the territory. There has been some raids into neighboring Missouri counties, too. I don't condone the plundering and horse-stealing of these Kansas men, but they have helped slaves escape Missouri by their raids. They've been nicknamed Jay-hawkers, because they are as ragged as jays and hungry as hawks.

For family news here, my nephew William James married Lucinda Shields on March 22 in Franklin. They started their romance when the Kennedy and Shields families moved to Kansas. When things calmed down this year, Lucinda's father consented to the marriage. I hope they can travel back to Ohio sometime so Lucinda can meet William James' siblings.

Thinking about our move to Kansas reminds me that it has been two years since we left Ohio. Time stood still while we held our breath during the troubles. Can I exhale and start over? Due to the problems here, I haven't felt at ease to call this "home" yet. I pray this territory will finally open up its arms this spring and welcome us to the land.

I hope you and your family are well. I promise my next letter will have warmer and better news.

Waiting for spring,

Margaret

P.S. As I was finishing this letter, Collins stopped by on his way home from town because there was a package at the post office for me. Thank you for all the seeds you sent! I was like a little girl in a candy shop when I saw what was in the package. I laid the packets out on the table in imaginary garden rows, rearranging as I dreamed of the fresh succulent vegetables and sweet-smelling flowers I'll be harvesting this summer. Your generosity was the ray of sunshine I've been needing. Thank you for renewing my spirit.

Tuesday, July 28, 1857
Douglas County, Kansas Territory

Dear Phoebe,

Life on my homestead has reached a hectic pace as crops mature. My farm is finally getting into production. I'm outside every morning hoeing weeds, cutting hay, or harvesting produce from the garden. My dress is soaking wet with sweat from the steamy Kansas sun by the end of the day, but I don't mind this year. My skin is sunburned brown, my bare feet are tough, and sometimes my joints are aching, but I'm happy. Seeing my crops grow thick and healthy has been a huge balm and relief to my soul.

The little patch of sod wheat yielded about twenty-seven bushels to the acre. By the size of the new ears, I predict we'll have an excellent stand of corn due to this spring's moisture. Oats planted late this spring are cut, bundled, and stacked, waiting to be threshed.

The boys have worked together to harvest the crops on each farm. On many occasions I've baked extra bread and pies in the morning and gone over to whomsoever's farm they were at on that particular day and helped serve the food. Being free of little ones, it is easy for me to move around and help where needed.

Tom plowed up a half-acre plot for my garden this year. I realize I haven't planted that much space in a dozen years, but I'm not going to let my family run out of food this winter like the last two. I took care and planted the above-ground plants with the new moon cycle and the underground ones with the old.

Leander predicts I'll have so much to harvest and store this fall that he'll have to dig a storage pit under half of our 160 acres to store it all. I told him to start digging because I want a cellar this year for my preserves.

Pumpkins, corn, and beans, will be dried out in the sun and stored in muslin bags hanging from my new cellar beams. We've already made fruit leather from wild plums and mulberries. I cook them to a paste and smear it on boards, which are laid by the fire to dry the mixture. When we need a fruit filling for a pie, we reheat one of these dry leathers with water to make it juicy again.

I'm almost embarrassed to say how I've secured pork for this winter. I bartered with a bachelor neighbor who misses his mother's cooking. He was over helping us one day, and of course stayed for dinner. The young man said my pie was so good he'd trade anything for one on his table every week. We struck a quick deal at the table with a handshake and another piece of pie. I got him to deliver three young pigs over here with the promise that I will make him a pie every Friday for the next six months. Looking over my growing garden, I hope he loves pumpkin.

The territory is bustling with positive activity this summer. Emigrants are flooding the territory now that the borders are open. The newspaper estimated that 30,000 people have entered the area so far this year. They expect nearly 100,000 by the end of 1857. The California Road never seems to be without traffic. Some people can find unclaimed land in this area, but most are pushing on west of Douglas County.

Everyone migrating from the States has heard of Lawrence, Kansas, because of last year's problems, and they head there first to see the town where the war was fought. Town lots are changing hands in a few days, usually at a profit. A four-story brick hotel is being built on the site of the old Free State Hotel. Downtown is rapidly changing into a cluster of brick stores ready to supply the emigrants with their supplies as they head westward.

Franklin, having the California Road as its main street, has been booming this year, too. Because it's longer a proslavery hangout, businesses are erecting establishments as fast as they can plane lumber at the mills. Franklin now boasts forty buildings, a two-story frame hotel, a general store, hardware stores, a blacksmith shop, sawmill, (of course saloons), and about four hundred residents. Three stagecoach lines pass through town, for it is a pickup point connecting Westport and the West.

John Pieratt has formed a partnership with a Dr. R.L. Williams. They are building a stone general store in Franklin. John's partner also practices medicine in the area. Our William James is working with Dr. Williams, building a new steam lumber mill on the east side of town for him.

The Williams family arrived in March. They left Illinois last fall, but when they arrived at the border, bands were raiding Kansas, so they stopped for the winter in Cass County, Missouri. I believe they met John Pieratt's brother, James, who settled in Missouri, and so looked up the Pieratts here when they arrived in the territory. They are both from Kentucky and have the same background and feelings about the slave situation, so Williams and Pieratt hit it off.

Deborah Pieratt was happy to hear news about their family in Missouri from them. It has been a tense year for her, with family on both sides of the border. Deborah has been a big comfort to Mrs. Williams, who through all this had to bury a baby boy in the cemetery, right after arriving here.

Did I ever mention that Franklin was started by the graveyard? A small daughter died as a family traveled west along the California Road, and the father buried her on a little hilltop. Unable to leave, the grieving parents built a home and were the first settlers in what became Franklin.

That sadly reminds me of my newest grandchild in Ohio, whom I may never meet. I still find it hard to imagine Sarah as a married woman with a baby. Please give little Charles a grandmother hug from me the next time you see them.

I've thought of Sarah often this month because we're quilting her Star and Cross quilt top that we brought with us two years ago. I finally obtained some wool for the inside batting, and feel I can finish it without the quilt getting stolen. I kept it hidden during the raids.

After the supper dishes are done we sit outside in the evening breeze to stitch until the light fades. On occasion, some of my other daughters have come over to help on it. I can't tell you how nice it is to be able to do normal work again.

I hope you are having a pleasant season, also.

Content with the hot Kansas summer,

Margaret

Wednesday, December 23, 1857
Douglas County, Kansas Territory

Dear Phoebe,

I know I have already written you this month with season's greetings, but I need to "talk" over the situation here. It is worth the cost of postage twice this month. At least I know this note will not reach you until after the holidays, so it won't spoil your holiday time.

My neighbor is over for his weekly pie and is talking to the boys about the latest election. They are arguing politics, and it is getting on my nerves. As it is almost Christmas, I am trying to stay in the peaceful spirit, but I'm at the point where I'm ready to bang a few heads with my rolling pin. I decided it was best to retire to the corner of the room and slash out with my pen instead.

Both the proslavery and free-state sides have been having conventions, complete with speeches, arguments, and elections all year. A census was taken to see how many legal people were in the state to vote, but the census books got into a few Missouri counties for registration and were conveniently forgotten to be circulated into certain Kansas free-state counties. The October election for a state constitution finally favored the free-state side, except for fraud in a few counties, which Governor Walker threw out. But the federal government failed to recognize the vote, almost causing the breakout of war again here. The free-staters refused to cast their ballots in the second this month, so the vote was obviously one-sided. Walker resigned, for he couldn't help the true feelings of the people and James Denver has succeeded into the governor's position now. Meetings are supposed to adjourn tomorrow until January 4. We'll see what happens next.

Sometimes I think the men don't decide anything on purpose just so they can keep up arguing for the pleasure of it. I firmly believe that if women had the right to vote, the matter would have been settled two years ago. So much time and energy have been wasted on the feuding that if it doesn't stop soon, our move will be for nothing.

Emigrants will stop coming to a place that is in constant turmoil. If the fledging towns wither away, we'll be stuck out on

51

the prairie all by ourselves, with land we cannot sell or profit from. Without markets to sell our grains, stores to buy supplies, churches to worship in, or schools to educate our children, what good is our rich Kansas soil?!

This fall I purchased a copy of the first map ever drawn for Douglas County. The paper cost me one dollar, but it was worth it because it shows my name on my quarter of land. Will it be the only thing I have left of my venture into Kansas farming if the territory collapses?

Seeing fireworks in December,

Margaret

New Arrivals

Saturday, January 23, 1858
Douglas County, Kansas Territory

Dear Phoebe,

Today's snow has tapered off to flurries, but it was still bitterly cold to do chores this evening. I'm sitting by the fire, smoking my clay pipe, trying to warm my old bones and catch up on the news and letters.

I've been reading about the financial panic that hit in the East this fall. Mired in our own territorial drama, the newspaper has not allotted much space for the subject until recently. Sounds like the States were hit hard by the economic calamities. The article said banks failed, businesses and railroads faced bankruptcy, land values dropped, and unemployment grew. Although it slightly affected Lawrence, I'm sure you felt the repercussions more in Ohio.

The newspaper editor guesses there won't be as many emigrants to our territory this year due to the national disaster. I'm not surprised that things happening so far away have an effect on us out on the prairie.

It sure holds true when it comes to Washington, D.C. In January, all free-staters were elected to the territorial offices, and the proslavery constitution was voted down. Of course, that didn't mean admission to the Union. President Buchanan, taking the Southern ground, is urging Congress to accept the constitution anyway. I wonder if we will ever become a state at the rate we're going. I'm trying to ignore politics and get on with life here, but sometimes it won't leave you alone.

Salina is sitting beside me sewing the last of her Evening Star quilt blocks together. We'll put it in the quilt frame Monday and start stitching the batting and back to the top. She turned seventeen on January 9, so it is time we get her trunk of quilts ready.

We also need to make new clothes for her changing figure. Her skirts and petticoats are too short and blouses are too tight.

She does not have a beau yet, but she has had her share of crushes on local boys. I sense her recent favorite is Belvard Pieratt because she insisted we shop in his family's store for the quilt batting, in hopes that he would wait on us.

It makes me feel old that my youngest child is of marrying age. What will I do when all of the children are out of my house?

I realize you are in the same situation, but at least you have Maggie for a few more years.

I miss Hugh more than ever when thinking of it. Instead of growing old with my husband, I'll be all alone. I still pine about leaving his grave, but when I look back and question my moving here, it was the right decision. I can always walk down the road in either direction and play with my lively grandchildren. That is better than staying in the past and visiting the stillness of the grave.

There have been offers of marriage since I moved to the territory, but I've declined them all. All these bachelors want is for someone to cook their meals and wash their clothes. And if they want anything else, they better look for a bride half my age.

Please tell Maggie that I held her new nephew, Alonzo Birk, this week. William James and Lucinda are adjusting to parenthood since his birth on the 5th. It is sad that William James' mother, Hannah, isn't alive to see her new grandson. I guess I'll just have to fill the role of the Kennedy grandmother for little Alonzo.

I will close for now. After I warm the bed with the hot hearth stone, I'm crawling in.

Dreaming of babies, past and present,

Margaret

Saturday, May 15, 1858
Douglas County, Kansas Territory

Dear Phoebe,

The warm sunlight baths my skin, soaking out the shivers of the past winter. I know I pester Salina to wear her sunbonnet to protect her face, but I have mine off while I sit outside writing. My skin is no longer young, so it doesn't matter.

Spring feels like it is finally here to stay. In this kind of weather I hate to be indoors where it still feels cold and damp, like the house has not warmed up out of its winter chill yet.

But I shouldn't complain about this last winter. We've been much more comfortable since we moved into the new house. Shake siding on the outside and plastered walls on the inside make a big difference during cold weather. Everything stays cleaner and warmer with the plank floor. The small room on the west side gives Salina and me more privacy and room than when we had to use the quilt to divide off our bed from my sons. Sunshine floods through the three windows, giving better light and a good view.

Next I want a porch on the side of the house. I didn't have one on my Ohio house, but there are homes here that do. Having people from several areas of the States has brought different kinds of construction to the territory. I've seen many things from neighbors I want to use in my farm buildings.

When I finished the chores this afternoon, I took a stroll down the road just to stay in the sun and observe the neighbor's progress in planting. It was my annual tuning into the new season.

After being dull and drab for months, the prairie is bursting with color and life. Fresh soft green grass is overtaking last year's dead stiff mat. Before I know it, the prairie hay in the meadow will be waist high and ready to cut.

Wildflowers are poking up from the mass of native grass. Tiny yellow buttercups only six inches tall nestle beside the tall bluestem. A pocket of tall purple sweet rocket caught my eye in the distance. There are so many flowers here in the wild compared to my old home. I suppose it is because all the land in Ohio was turned into farmland decades ago, and many of the wildflowers were crowded out.

When I visited Deborah Pieratt yesterday, I asked her if she knew the name of a particular flower I had seen on the way over to her house. We walked down by the Wakarusa to see if we could find the plant I was talking about, and there lay a blanket of dainty light blue violets near the bank of the river. I commented that I hadn't seen that color around here before. She said these violets came from Kentucky. The spring after her sister, Ann, died, Deborah sprinkled seed she brought with her onto the dirt mound of the grave. That way she would always remember the spot.

Deborah seldom mentions her sister, but when we were by the grave, she told me bits and pieces of their lives, growing up in Kentucky, and about their trip in '54. They were among the first to cross into the new territory. It would have been vastly different from my trip, because we came a year later and had several women in our group. They were two women alone on the newly opened prairie. And then Deborah was without female companionship when her sister died.

I shivered when Deborah told me how Ann died of consumption on a cold winter day. They buried her wrapped in a quilt she had just finished. My first thought was that it was a waste of needed bedding, since a dead person doesn't need a blanket. Deborah explained that it was Ann's wedding quilt that she labored on before she died, and she couldn't bear the two to be apart. I understood, because I tucked special items in my children's caskets. Even when the person is dead, we still want to comfort them.

Just now there was a different song in the air besides the meadowlark I have become accustomed to. I think it was a robin. It must have a nest down in the trees along the creek. Songbirds were absent when we first arrived, but they are slowly moving in.

Trains are doing the same thing. Tracks have been laid into the territory. The first train traveled from St Joseph, Missouri, to Atchison on the 12th. Lawrence will be connected to the Eastern states in the near future. Maybe I can travel back to Ohio to see family when it happens.

Have you heard that gold has been found in our western mountain border? Rumors have circulated since last fall, when a group heading back to their home state of Georgia told of finding gold around the Cherry Creek Divide in our territory. They displayed samples of the dust in St. Louis, causing several groups to head west as soon as the weather warmed up.

This spring, an Indian who lives north of the Kansas River also showed nuggets to a Lawrence butcher when he sold cattle to the man. The Indian found the gold in a stream while traveling that region as Colonel Sumner's military guide. Wagons from Lawrence are heading down the Santa Fe Trail to follow the Arkansas River west to explore the Indian's claim. The California gold strike of '49 caused the country to go crazy. I wonder if finding gold on our border will do the same.

Although I hate to go inside, it is time to start supper. The boys have been working in the fields today and will arrive home with huge appetites. Salina took out an afternoon lunch of coffee and rolls to tide them over, but they will wolf down a big meal this evening. The weather, and the promise of a calm year, has made them enthusiastic again. But aren't farmers always optimistic?

Please go by my old farm and see if the apple trees are in bloom. I miss the sight and smell of those pink clouds in the spring. The scent was so strong I could smell it from the house. I was hoping my apple sapling would be big enough to produce a small amount of fruit this year, but a late frost killed the few blooms it produced. Maybe next year.

Optimistic about spring,

Margaret

Thursday, August 26, 1858
Douglas County, Kansas Territory

Dear Phoebe,

I plan to go into town tomorrow to trade my butter for groceries, so I must get your letter penned today so I can mail it at the same time. Now is my chance to write because a late afternoon thunderstorm has come, causing me to abandon my garden and head for dry shelter.

As we picked produce, I kept an eye on a thunderhead cloud as it reached enormous proportions this last hour. The hollyhocks edging my garden were waving as the wind got stronger, then they rocked to a stop. The breeze had stilled suddenly, giving the eerie feeling of a pressure front about to hit. We were ready to head for the underground cellar, but then the mood of the storm switched and brought only rain.

When bad weather hits Kansas, we pay attention. One never knows when the storm will produce hail or a cyclone. I pick vegetables every day but Sunday because I don't want any of my winter supply to be wiped out by bad weather.

Today we worked on beets. Most of this root crop will be stored whole, but I wanted to put up some beet relish. Salina laments she will never get the beet stains off her hands. (There is a neighborhood social Saturday night.) But I bet she'll try to add color to her cheeks with the red juice before she leaves the house.

In your last letter you asked about my new grandbabies and the latest territorial news.

The proslavery constitution was put to the vote of the territory *again* on the 2nd. Kansas voted against it *again*, like we did last year. This time Congress added a land grant bill, thinking we would be gullible enough to vote for the land issue, forgetting that the proslavery constitution would be automatically approved with our vote at the same time.

The land bill was tempting because it would have given us statehood immediately. Now Congress says the territory has to have more residents before we can be considered. That's just fine.

It would be better to be a free territory indefinitely than a proslavery state forever.

No, I haven't heard much about the Lincoln and Douglas campaign debates going on for the Illinois senate seat. Our newspaper has said little about it because we have enough politics to keep its pages full. Being in Ohio, I'm sure you'll hear more about the run between the two men than we will.

Well, here I am rambling on about the territory and everything else, avoiding family news that you'd want to hear but that I cringe to write.

Bridge's daughter, Josephine, died on the 16th. She died one day short of her first birthday. Even though I've lost children of my own, I think it is harder to watch one's child lose one of his own. There is so little you can do, because time is the only thing that will help.

I loaned Bridge his father's wood plane to make the coffin. The tiny box was made from walnut lumber cut from river timber that Bridge had planned to make into new furniture for his expanding family.

We debated whether to bury Josephine in the Lawrence or Franklin cemeteries, but then decided to start our own plot. We picked a spot north of Bridge's house, close to the Wakarusa. All the Kennedys that moved to Kansas, and the ones yet to be born, will die someday. Although it is hard to think about, it is comforting to know we will still be together in the afterlife. Maybe soon I'll be laid to rest next to my granddaughter.

One bright note is that our family still increases with Nettie's healthy baby, also named Josephine, born on the 4th of July. I guess we could expect that with this patriotic family.

I believe this is enough news for you to absorb in this letter. The sky has cleared, so I'll head back outside to see how much rain we got.

Thinking about my Josephines,

Margaret

Sunday, September 19, 1858
Douglas County, Kansas Territory

Dear Phoebe,

Could you see the comet?! I've spent the last hour outside in the crisp air, gazing at the heavens. How often in one's lifetime does one get to gaze upon such a wonder? I may never get the chance again.

When the glow was spotted Tuesday night, we thought it was a fire somewhere in the distance. Wednesday the word spread around what it was, so neighbors were out on the hilltops that night. We had no idea how long it would be visible.

We packed children and pots of coffee in the wagons after supper and headed out for the evening. The bluffs to the west of us blocked the best view, so we traveled to the top of Bridge's land. My younger grandchildren slept through the night drama, but I think the older children will remember it.

It was visible a few hours after sundown, right above the west horizon. The fiery ball had two narrow tails shooting straight up, and one wide tail slightly curving to the right like a graceful bird's feather.

I've looked every night since it appeared when the sky has been clear. The comet was still there tonight, but I didn't think it was brilliant as Wednesday. To think that this same comet has passed by the earth during my ancestors' time and may be seen again by a descendant of mine. Will they realize that their great-great grandmother stood outside during a September night to share it with them?

Salina had the attention of a certain young man that night and barely noticed the luminous heavens. She is starry-eyed over Alonzo Hindman, a boy from Ohio, whose family staked a claim in the Willow Springs Township south of us. I don't know if they are serious yet, but Salina is enjoying his company more than mine, or the comet's, recently.

They met at a neighborhood social a few months ago. Alonzo lives several miles from us but has made excuses to show up in our area many times since. Whenever he is heading for Lawrence, he stops and asks if she would like to ride along.

The boys were overly protective of Salina at first. Before they had gotten to know Alonzo, they questioned Salina about her whereabouts when she was out with him. My sons were worse than I was.

Salina has shown a new sense of awareness to tasks around the house, asking questions about cooking and housekeeping. Do you suppose they have talked about marriage, and it has dawned on Salina what kind of serious responsibility a commitment of vows would make?

At the last social my three unmarried children were lovestruck. Matchmaking is in the air as the comet passes our region. I wonder how many thoughts wished upon that giant star will come true for my young ones.

I hope your eyes were scanning the sky tonight.

With star-struck wishes,

Margaret

Monday, November 15, 1858
Douglas County, Kansas Territory

Dear Phoebe,

I was so surprised when little Maggie walked in my cabin door! I knew that William James planned to pick up his brother John in Indiana and visit siblings in Ohio before they swung back through Illinois to help the Duttons move to Kansas. I didn't expect their little tag-a-long sister. I know I shouldn't think of her that way anymore. At twelve, she is spurting toward womanhood. She had changed so much since I last saw her three years ago.

When I asked why she left Ohio, Maggie just smiled, saying she wanted to experience the new frontier with her brothers. Did she read my letters to you? She mentioned things I assumed she wouldn't know about! I know the war between the two groups here in Kansas has calmed down, but I didn't expect you to let her come anyway.

Maggie stayed with me a few days, then I took her back to William James and Lucinda's new farm. We stopped in Franklin at Pieratt's store so Maggie could met part of the Pieratt family. The three older boys were there stocking shelves. Deborah, the girls, and little John happened to be in town at the same time. Sarah and George Ann Pieratt are close enough in age to Maggie that they struck up a friendship right way.

I hadn't seen Deborah Pieratt for a while. I noticed a marked change in her weight and energy. When I asked, she just said the weather was getting her down, but I'm afraid she is showing signs of something more serious. Because you know Deborah so well through my letters, I thought I would pass on my concern.

At William James' house, Maggie dragged everything out of her trunk to show me what she had brought along. There was a story to go with each item.

Something strengthened between us when she pulled out the quilt I had given her before I left Ohio. While at my house, Maggie spent most of the time with Salina, going through her trousseau and talking about her wedding plans. Maggie was almost shy with me, for we have been apart for so long. With the quilt she felt close to me again.

She burst with pride when she showed me her first quilt top, of the Ohio Star design. In the center was the pattern block she used to get started. It's been years, but I recognized it was the quilt block that Hannah was working on before she died. Did Maggie know that? She said her sister Mary Ann gave it to her.

Mary Ann must have also given her Matilda's sewing basket. I recognized the initials on the basket lid immediately. Going through Maggie's things sparked a lot of memories of my own children. I dabbed my eyes more than once that afternoon.

When Maggie pulled out her Bible, she changed the subject, telling me she had helped her brothers plant a living fence of black locust trees around the graveyard that holds her parents and siblings. Maggie was taken aback when I thanked her for that gesture, explaining that my loved ones are buried there also. That's when she grew misty-eyed, opened up her Bible, and unfolded a piece of paper that she had stuck inside. A dried cluster of tiny tree leaves were flattened between the pages. For some reason, she had felt compelled to save a twig from one of the trees. I think it puzzled her a bit, because Hannah and Michael were people she does not remember, or feel close to. Except for a few brief recollections, I fear her memories of them are fading as she gets older.

I told her about my thimble of soil I brought with me to memorialize the place that was dear to my heart. It helped her understand why she wanted something to remember the place and time where she last saw her family's graves. I hope Maggie treasures her keepsake, because it will keep her parents in her heart.

While she was digging through her belongings, bits of her trip from Ohio slowly came out. Her comment was that it was a cold walk, but by the stories she told, I think she enjoyed the trip and the scenery. Many times the trips are easier on the children than the adults, who have all the responsibilities. Sounds like she ganged up with Elvira Dutton against the four Dutton brothers more than once.

The Duttons are now my neighbors directly to the east. Asa, Scott, and Collins traded land between them. Scott has had a hard time adjusting to Louise's unexpected death. Cate took over the mothering of their only child, so Scott and little Jenny moved in with Cate and Collins, leaving their home empty. Duttons wanted to be in Kennedy Valley and needed a house, so Scott's dugout was the obvious choice.

Mary Dutton insists that she won't stay in the dugout very long. I told her that's the warmest place in the valley during the winter, to enjoy it while she has it, and to expect company if the temperature becomes severe. They plan to build a new house next spring.

Other than getting reacquainted with old friends, we're getting ready for winter. The heavy rains we got this summer were a mixed blessing. Wheat and oats yielded poorly, most consumed with rust and blight. But the moisture boosted the corn up to one hundred bushels to an acre in some areas. We're still husking corn in the fields, myself included. (And I've got the chapped hands and stiff back to prove it!)

Tom had to build another bin to hold the corn, for we crib it in the ear. It has been selling between 25 to 40 cents a bushel this fall, but after our last winters, I want to make sure we have enough food to last us through the worst months before I sell any of the crop.

We've been saving and shedding the best of the husks for Salina's bed ticking. It makes a superior bed to prairie grass or feathers, so now is the time to get her mattress ready for her new home.

I'm sure you are feeling the loss of Maggie, but rest assured she is happy and adjusting. There are enough Kennedys here that she'll be well taken care of. I'll watch over her and write you of her adventures.

You've done a good job raising Maggie, Phoebe. Thank you for letting her come to Kansas.

Happy to see my niece,

Margaret

Kansas Gold

Tuesday, February 22, 1859
Douglas County, Kansas Territory

Dear Phoebe,

Family matters in both states have affected you and me this month. Necessity has called for tolerance in me. I hope you have weathered the changes.

My condolences to your family on the death of your brother-in-law, Joseph Curless. I trust he left his family and yours provided for.

I think you should know that we went to court yesterday to protect John, Maggie, and their interests. Since Joseph was the legal guardian of Hannah's children, we were afraid that another guardian would be appointed by a Brown County judge in Ohio if we didn't take immediate action. Both children wanted to stay in Kansas, so William James has been appointed their principal guardian. R.L. Williams and John Pieratt were named as secondary guardians in the document. It pains me that I couldn't be listed as guardian also, but the law doesn't allow women to do so.

Well, my youngest has left the nest. Salina and Alonzo were married recently in Lawrence. I didn't realize until she was gone how much I have counted on Salina for companionship and help since we left Ohio. I questioned their plan, for they are both so young, but I gave her my consent anyway. I did my best to prepare her for married life, and she felt confident to leave. I can only hope she and Alonzo get to share a long happy life together with the joy of healthy children. Every woman faces unknown trials out in the prairie of life.

We celebrated the occasion with a large family gathering before the couple moved to their new home beside Alonzo's parents. I won't see Salina very often, for they are not in our valley. Tom and Leander were in on their chivaree, and have seen them since their wedding day. I plan to go down this spring to help her start her garden. I'm staying away now because she needs to get adjusted to her new life without me.

It was a trial to round up enough things to start Salina's new household. Had we still been in Ohio, I would have had plenty of odds and ends for her. Her sisters and neighborhood women pitched in with sewing bees to get her clothes and quilts ready. Maggie was feeling left out, for she missed her sister Caroline's wedding in Ohio last month. Salina included her cousin in the preparations. I'm sure Maggie wrote more details about the wedding to you than I have.

Maggie ended up staying with me for a few days after the wedding. Do you suppose she and Salina planned this to ease my loss?

Feeling lonely,

Margaret

Thursday, June 30, 1859
Douglas County, Kansas Territory

Dear Phoebe,

We lost Deborah Pieratt to consumption on the 26th. She died one day short of her twentieth wedding anniversary. Over the spring months she wasted away to nothing. Finally there was no more air in her lungs to sustain her.

It is sad that so many pioneer women fight so many battles to keep their families safe, and then die of a disease that no amount of fighting will defeat.

John Pieratt has distanced himself from the family in his grief and is ignoring his children. The boys, ages eighteen to thirteen, spend most of their time at the store or in the field. Sarah, being the oldest girl at eleven, must care for the three younger ones and manage the household.

Yesterday Lucinda and her sister, Nancy Shields, and I went over to their house, trying to get the home organized for the Pieratt girls. Maggie went along to entertain the youngest Pieratts and Lucinda's baby.

I'm sure Deborah turned over in her grave, because we found the house to be in an unclean state, but it couldn't be helped. Everything from cellar shelves to bedding was cleaned and put back in order. Nancy volunteered to check on the girls every week to make sure they are coping with the household chores.

Before I left, Sarah handed me an envelope. On the outside was written, "Margaret, Please take care of this after I'm gone. Thank you for being such a good neighbor and friend." She was trying to tell me something in code, but I did not understand her plea until I shook the envelope. Stopping by the Wakarusa on my way home, I sprinkled violet seeds on her grave and watered them with my tears.

Missing my dear neighbors, near and far,

Margaret

Monday, August 15, 1859
Douglas County, Kansas Territory

Dear Phoebe,

What a difference a few months can make. Word spread that a big vein of gold was found in the mountains, causing another surge of gold fever. This find was northwest of Pikes Peak on Clear Creek.

It was estimated that 150,000 people have crossed the Great Plains this summer, with about a third of them becoming "go-backs," people turning around before they ever see the mountains. Over 600 wagons left Omaha in one week alone for the gold fields.

Thousands lost their jobs in the fall of '57, when the factories closed Back East. Still not finding work, many of those people have gone crazy at the notion of striking it rich. Some of the smart ones are heading to the western border to set up businesses in the new towns of Auraria and Denver, at the base of the mountains, and Black Hawk and Central City, nestled up near the gold fields.

Towns along the Missouri-Kansas border are cashing in selling supplies to these greenhorn travelers. I wish half these items were available four years ago, when we were trying to settle here.

One of their best-selling items is the *Handbook to the Gold Fields of Nebraska and Kansas*. I thumbed through a copy once, and I doubt the writers ever set foot in this territory the way the lay of the land was described. The book will become campfire tinder by the middle of the traveler's trip when he finds it is useless.

The *Herald of Freedom* listed the route in the newspaper. From Lawrence it is 556 miles to the gold fields by way of the Smoky Hill Fork. People are heading straight west on that river rather than going south along the Arkansas River.

Family groups have been absent so far. Men are heading out to claim their stakes and establish their homes before moving the family. On foot, with a gun slung over the shoulder and a knapsack hanging on the end, or pushing a wheelbarrow, they head out alone or in groups.

Heard about a few ingenious men trying to cross the prairie by wind wagons. Instead of horses pulling the wagon, they rig sails to the bed to catch the prairie breeze. They can travel over fifty miles a day but crash easily if they are caught in a whirlwind. There are no accounts of one making it the whole way because they have all wrecked before reaching their destination.

I've seen a few determined women pulling handcarts—many clothed in bloomer costumes. Some are dressed in fancy silk attire with their faces painted. They are soiled doves going to make a sinful living among the miners.

The people with money are shelling out $200 to travel to the western border by stagecoach. I wouldn't call it luxury traveling, being packed tight in a dusty, smelly coach, but it is the fastest way to get there. The stagecoaches roll continuously day and night for six days before they reach Denver.

The New York editor, Horace Greeley, visited our area on his way out to observe the gold rush. Compared to the easy life he must lead in the East, he's in for a rough time, and a lot of fodder for his newspaper column.

Greeley was trying to start the National Republican Party in Kansas when he went through here. The goal is to organize this political party of freedom in every state and territory of the Union. Some of the old Free State Party who came in '55 are not so sure of the new group. At least the party is headed in the right direction.

Your last letter told of fair weather in Ohio. The spring here was a mire of cold and mud until the rains stopped in May. Summer heated up so fast that now we pray for a thundercloud to drop some moisture instead of threatening with gales of dust. Roads are like baked brick in this sweltering heat. The garden is stressed between the high temperatures and lack of soil moisture.

We harvested a good crop of wheat and oats right when it turned hot. Now I worry about the heat and lack of rain for the corn crop. The ears are not filled out with even rows of kernels on the stunted stalks I've checked so far.

I hope we get some rain before we need to start planting our fall crop of wheat. Are we headed for a drought? I have consulted the Old Farmer's Almanac, but it doesn't give a clue of any unusual weather for this fall.

There are definite changes in my household. Leander married Amanda Todd on July 29 and they are living with me. (Her family lives east of Bridge's.) I have signed over my quarter of land to them.

We added another room onto the house for more privacy for the newlyweds. I think Amanda was slightly intimidated by my running the house, but we're getting better working together. Some household jobs I've turned over to her, happy to have the relief.

Tom has set September 11 as his wedding date to Martha Nolan. They'll set up housekeeping across the road from us.

Life is different for me with my children married. Maybe it is time for you and me to "see the elephant" as the phrase goes. Maybe we should head west to see the sights, seek our fortune, or find more boys to cook for!

From the old mother of the grooms,

Margaret

Tuesday, October 25, 1859
Douglas County, Kansas Territory

Dear Phoebe,

Amanda has the fresh pork roasting on the turnspit, potatoes boiling in the kettle, and bread baking in the Dutch oven nestled in the hot coals. I'm sitting here recuperating from the annual fall butchering of our hogs. I did not put up any fuss when Amanda said she would take care of tonight's meal.

I am tired. Now that I've stopped for the day, my shoulders and knees ache. I'm not sure if it is from lifting heavy crocks of meat or grandchildren.

Everyone came over here for the day. The adults worked from dawn until last light cleaning, cutting, and packing the meat. The big kettle we used for making soap and heating wash water was rigged up to scald the carcasses. Long planks were sent up for work tables. With a gang of workers, it went smoothly.

Each family took home a quantity of meat to smoke and pack in salt for the winter. Of course the best part is fresh pork we'll have for a few days. My mouth is watering with anticipation of tonight's meal. Tomorrow's breakfast will be brown bread drenched with milk gravy and topped with crisp fried side pork. Can you smell the aroma coming from the skillet?

I enjoyed the day's worth of gossip and news that goes with the gathering. It took our minds off the hard work.

The main talk was about John Brown's raid on the Federal arsenal at Harper's Ferry, Virginia this month. The newspapers reported his plan was to seize the weapons built at the factory and arm the slaves to force their freedom from the slaveholders. He did this last winter in Missouri, but on a much smaller scale. Brown was captured when the slaves in Virginia didn't join his attack. They were probably more afraid of him than of their masters! Now Brown is on trial for treason against the state of Virginia and for inciting a slave uprising. We figure he'll be sentenced to hang for the crimes.

I always worried when Brown was in our area. His hatred of slavery drove him mad. If you didn't think like him, your life was in jeopardy. Brown's cause was righteous, but his method of winning it cost many lives. I admired his courage because it loosened the roots of slavery, but I doubted his wisdom. His favorite Old Testament reading was, "Without the shedding of blood, there is no remission of sins."

I wonder how his latest actions will affect the troubles brewing between the North and the South.

At least in our territory, politics is going better this fall. The new constitution drafted this summer was passed without bloodshed in legal voting. This time it was the Republicans versus the Democrats, instead of the free-staters voting against the proslavers. Now we have to wait for Congress to vote on it.

I've saved the biggest gossip for last. The neighborhood was surprised when John Pieratt married Nancy Shields last month. With a large young family to take care of, I thought he would remarry someday. We just didn't expect it to be six weeks after Deborah's death. I guess John figured it was best to keep Nancy around after she organized their lives.

Maggie has visited the Pieratts often after Deborah's death. She knows firsthand how unsettling it is to lose a parent. She thought the girls were resigned, but not happy about their father's decision. All things considered, I think Deborah would be glad her children are being taken care of. Maybe Nancy's taking over of the family was planned.

We need to set the table, so it is time to close this letter.

Hope you have your cellar full of meat for winter. Today I've reminisced about the fall butcherings we did together years ago. Try as I might with different combinations of seasonings, I still can't get my pork sausage to taste as good as yours. I'd love to have a piece of that again.

Ready for supper,

Margaret

Thursday, December 15, 1859
Douglas County, Kansas Territory

Dear Phoebe,

I'm proud and relieved to write that after five years, the territory has finally set up a public school system for our children. Our informal Kennedy Valley School, will be called Pleasant Valley District, No. 14. The session is to begin January 16.

Asa Dutton deeded an acre of land for the school site. This month the men have been erecting a 14 by 16 foot log schoolhouse. As it's only forty rods from our house, I've gotten involved, supplying hot coffee and food for the workers. If I was younger, I'd have helped put up the logs myself.

By Eastern standards it is very crude with its rough unplaned oak flooring and backless benches instead of desks. I wouldn't have put the door on the north side, but that way it faces the road. A four-paned window on both the east and west sides of the building offer light to the interior.

I'm not sure the little wood stove in the center of the building will prevent frosted toes and ears on the children, but we can hope for mild weather during the months school convenes. I'm confident the district will keep growing and better schoolhouses will be built in the future. At least we are finally getting the support we need for our children's education.

I worry about Joe's three deaf children, though. They need special schooling, but there is no such place in the territory. Sending them to a school in the States might help them, but Joe cannot afford that, nor would the family want to be separated. Matilda and Emma aren't old enough for school yet, but will be soon.

I look forward to the Christmas season this year. Even though we ended up with a low yield of corn, I plan to deliver small baskets of food to special families in the neighborhood.

I've invited all the grandchildren to stop in after the Christmas Day church service to receive their special gift from me. I tatted a tiny lace star for each of them. I added a thread loop on them so they can be hung. With the addition of Joe's baby boy,

Oran, and William James' girl, Mary Caroline, this year, I've kept busy getting these done on time.

I send the blessing of the season to you and yours. May you have a prosperous new year also.

Getting ready for Christmas,

Margaret

Grandmother's Choice

Friday, April 13, 1860
Douglas County, Kansas Territory

Dear Phoebe,

Today is the last day of school for this session. I've watched my grandchildren trudge up and down the trail in front of my house for three months. I plan to have warm cookies ready when they pass by on their way home.

It is pleasant today, so I'm sitting out on the porch, smelling the fragrant spring air. The wildflowers I dug from the prairie five years ago are greening up around the house. The Kentucky violets are blooming now. In another month the wild roses will unfurl their reddish pink petals and cast off their scent.

Looks like my apple tree across the road might be in early bloom this year. The buds are starting to swell. I wonder what our lack of spring moisture will do to the crop. I have yet to get more than a bushel of apples off that tree.

Spring is slow greening up our country because of the lack of snow during our winter. We need rain soon, or the ground moisture will be depleted before we get the seed in and germinated.

The schoolchildren are outside for their recess. Since they are close by, I can't miss the sights and sounds of over forty children across the field.

Schoolmaster Stubbs earned his pay this year with so many children. I liked teaching small groups, but now there are more children in our neighborhood than I'd care to handle at one time.

In some ways I'm still teaching. Sometimes Lucy has brought our younger grandchildren to my house before school is out, so they walk home with their older siblings. We're teaching a simple sign language to all the children so the deaf cousins don't feel left out when they are all together. It is best to get them started at an early age.

Looks like we may finally become a state. The House of Representatives voted to admit Kansas to the Union. Now we have to wait for the Senate's vote. Topeka has been selected to be the capital. After all the votes we have been through, I'm not holding my breath. The state will celebrate when it finally happens.

Politics has been on everyone's mind, this being a presidential election year. Even though Abraham Lincoln campaigned in our territory last December, I think the Republicans of Kansas will vote for William Seward if our statehood passes in time.

Have you heard about the new Pony Express mail line that started this month? It's the talk here, for it goes through Kansas. The company has set up relay stations between St. Joseph, Missouri and Sacramento, California, a distance of almost two thousand miles. The plan is to have a rider gallop from station to station, changing ponies and riders along the way, and get to Sacramento in ten days. I saw the advertisement in the newspaper, looking for "daring young men, preferably orphans" to risk the ride. The Pony Express was started to compete with the Butterfield Overland Mail. The first rider left on the 3rd, so the mail pouch should be in California today if they didn't have problems.

Before we know it, the territory between the two coasts will be settled and trains will run the whole width of the continent. Do you think it will happen in our lifetime?

Watching the change in the country,

Margaret

Sunday, July 8, 1860
Douglas County, Kansas Territory

Dear Phoebe,

We gathered at William James and Lucinda's today to celebrate upcoming birthdays and new births in the Kennedy family.

I thought I would expire from heat exhaustion before I got to their house. Gusts of wind filtered dust into my clothing and covered my perspiring face with a fine layer of grit. The summer heat wave continues to climb to unbearable temperatures. The air hangs so hot and heavy it is hard to breathe at times. This kind of weather is hard on man and beast.

Since I last wrote, Salina had her baby boy, Charles, and Amanda gave birth to Isabelle this week. Maggie was hoping the little girl would be born on her fourteenth birthday, but Isabelle was one day late. Leander's first child isn't very healthy, and this heat makes matters worse. I fear I will lose another grandchild soon.

Scott is marrying again next month, to Martha Woodruff. They knew each other in Ohio years ago, and got reacquainted when her family moved here.

Our nephew John was visiting before he left on his latest run. He is driving a wagon between Leavenworth and Denver for a freight company. So far he has crossed the territory twice this summer. As he is only eighteen, this job has been an education for him. The stories he told of sights on the trail and the new town of Denver made Nettie's little sons ready to ride shotgun for him. I know John witnessed tragedy and horror along the way, too, but he left those details out for the children's version.

A new wave of gold seekers, just like the heat, continues to travel through the territory. As this drought hangs on, more farmers are giving up their claims and heading west. This time family wagons are rambling through, with "Pikes Peak or Bust" written on their canvas tops. It has been estimated that eleven thousand wagons were on the road to Denver during May and June alone.

We've heard numerous tales of problems along the trail, but people keep coming. There is very little vegetation along the

Smoky Hill, so there has been a shortage of fuel and food at certain times of the season. Water varies from too much at swollen river crossings, to not enough at a sinkhole to water a horse.

There have been isolated problems with the Indians. I'm sure they think the white men are crazy looking for specks of gold in the dirt, but as long as the travelers keep moving and don't bother the buffalo, the Indians have left most of the gold seekers alone.

The unrelenting drought has taken a toll on the prairie. Stunted tree leaves, caked with dust, are falling off the trees as the small streams dry up. The ground is rock hard—like iron beneath our feet. The few crops here that sprouted this spring in the moisture-poor fields are withering as this drought continues. The corn grew a puny foot before the leaves turned gray and curled inward for lack of moisture. What's left of the dead stalks is being devoured by grasshoppers. The prairie grass stopped growing and turned dry. Prairie fires are a constant worry.

Here's another year to worry about our winter food supply. Sometimes I almost lose all hope. Everything seems to be a battle here.

Someone from our neighborhood made the comment, "Hell can't be hotter than Kansas." I hope I have led a good enough life that when I die I don't have to venture into Hades and this heat again.

Wishing for a cool breeze,

Margaret

Saturday, October 27, 1860
Douglas County, Kansas Territory

Dear Phoebe,

Thank you for your recent letter of birthday wishes. I always look forward to your news about home, friends, and family. They keep me connected to my past. Your continued faithful friendship through the years means a great deal to me.

I can't believe I am sixty years old today. When I was born on that little Ohio River island near Manchester, I bet my mother never imagined I would living out in the Great American Desert. The territory west of the Mississippi River had not been explored yet, and it was assumed only savages and buffalo could survive in that rough landscape.

Everyone is thinking the same thing now. It has been suggested that the territory should be turned back to the Indians. Thirty thousand people have left the territory, traveling east across the border that they fought so hard to cross in the first place.

By the middle of August everything was dried up—crops, trees, streams, wells, and cows. We have gone over a year without measurable rainfall. Wild geese are bypassing the area because there is no water to land on. Only the Kansas River has any water left. The Wakarusa is down to a trickle.

It is estimated that there is only enough food for half the territory's population. The States are starting to respond to our dire situation by shipping food to the territory. A carload of New England beans arrived at the Lawrence depot this week, but it won't curb the whole population's hunger through the winter.

We voted not to abandon our claims, because we knew the drought would not last forever. Besides, our land in Ohio is gone. Where could we go to keep together? California and Oregon were mentioned, but we have put so much of ourselves in this place. This time, due to the drought, we couldn't sell our land to have money to start over.

Since we have a large family to look after, we went in search of food ourselves. Will Curless took off with a wagon and four yoke of oxen to find staples. He had to go all the way to Des Moines, Iowa to find a ton of flour.

After he got back, he received word from family in Illinois that they were gathering up food they could spare after harvest. Will walked to Leavenworth, traveled from there to St. Joseph, Missouri by stagecoach, where he is supposed to catch the train to Illinois. We are painfully awaiting in destitute Kansas for his return with food.

I feel settled here after five years in the territory, but our situation is no better than the winter of '55. We are going into another winter with no food, and we're not a state yet. I'm old enough to know that there will always be good and bad times in a person's life, but it is hard to hold to faith when trials keep hitting again and again.

Feeling the decades today,

Margaret

Tuesday December 31, 1860
Douglas County, Kansas Territory

Dear Phoebe,

On the eve of the new year I'm sitting in my rocking chair in my usual spot by the fire. My only company tonight is the dog lying on the rug before my feet.

Leander and Amanda are out to see the new year in with friends. Even though the past year has been so bad for them with the baby's death and drought, they are optimistic again because Amanda is with child. Budding life puts a new perspective on everything.

I look at them and see me and Hugh at that age. That was forty years ago. What were our parents' thoughts when they saw us become parents and they were pushed back to being the older folk? Probably the same as me: hating to get old but glad the cycle of our family is being continued with another generation.

I am warm and cozy this evening because my family surprised me with a lap quilt to celebrate my sixth decade. I'm sure you knew about the surprise, for Sarah sent blocks from Ohio. The girls didn't get it done by my birthday, so they waited until Christmas, when the family was together.

How they got it pieced and quilted without me knowing it—or the grandchildren spilling the secret—is beyond me. Lucinda and Maggie quilted it together at their place so I wouldn't walk in on the process at one of my nearby children's home.

This quilt is also special because of the saving and scrimping they had to do in order to donate and buy the materials needed. Cate told me, "You've done that all your life for us, so we wanted to show our appreciation." I think this is the only quilt I own that I didn't do a stitch of work on!

They appropriately used the Grandmother's Choice design. Each daughter or daughter-in-law stitched her own children's names in the white space bars of the pattern, so each block is in a different handwriting stitch. Maggie did the block for Elizabeth's children. Nettie had her sixth child on the 13th of December, so that makes thirty grandchildren's names so far on my treasure. I only knew some of the babies a few hours or months, but all of their names are immortalized on this quilt. Made from a hodgepodge of scraps, it is as bright and colorful as the little ones it portrays. I recognize material from several dresses I made for the children and grandchildren over the years. Every evening since I received the quilt I've sat admiring it, tracing names with my fingers, thinking about the special little person each represents.

They left spaces to fill in later as more grandchildren arrive. I wonder, what will their names be, who will they look like, what will they accomplish in their lifetimes?

I also wonder what the territory of Kansas will do for these children. This place has not received its settlers with open arms. We have had to fight each step of the way. Will their children and grandchildren survive and flourish here, or move elsewhere?

Twice recently the Senate voted down the motion to consider the Kansas bill. The Southern senators are hampering our statehood. After five years of fruitless hard work and suffering, I wonder if I will ever see Kansas become a peaceful state in the Union.

Also, there is a bill in Congress to form the territory of Colorado. It would include land from the western part of our territory and change the Kansas and Nebraska boundaries. We're losing ground before we've gotten the chance to become a state.

The motto picked for Kansas is *Ad Astra per Aspera,* meaning "to the stars through difficulties." Don't you think that phrase is appropriate for the problems we've had? We've tried for years to become a star on the American flag, but have yet to succeed.

Who knows what will happen next round since South Carolina seceded from the Union this month. What if other Southern states follow? I wonder if the Union can divide up into two peaceful nations, or will people go to war to keep the states together? Abraham Lincoln is going to have his hands full when he takes over the presidential office next year. I wouldn't want to be in his shoes.

Reflection from the firelight shows droplets of water on the outside window pane. Soft rain has started to fall to the earth. I imagine it will change to sleet or snow as the cold comes on, but at this stage the gentle rain soothes my soul.

The rains came back in November, ending the sixteen-month drought. It was too late for this growing season, but it will help restore water in the creeks, rivers, and wells. We need to replenish the ground moisture for next year's planting. Will we get enough to do that, or is our late fall rain just a phantom that will dry up again when we need it?

Even though we have rich soil, farming continues to be a challenge in Kansas.

By my mantle clock it is almost the new year. I've spent the evening looking back over the 1850s, wondering if life is better here than in Ohio. I can't draw a simple conclusion. We'll see what the new decade brings for my family, our territory, and the Union. I still have hope that we made the right decision when our quest for land led us here.

I hope the new year is healthy and prosperous for you and your family. Please keep your Kansas relatives in your prayers.

Pondering the past, hoping for the future,

Margaret

P.S. I wish you could see my lap quilt. As I folded it up, I thought of Maggie again. On a top corner of the quilt back she stitched her initials—MJK, the date—October 27, 1860, and the outline of a thimble.

Ohio Rose

State of Ohio

Yankee Puzzle

Puss-in-Boots

Cleveland Tulip

Indian Trails

Log Cabin

Star and Cross

Evening Star

Ohio Star

*Dolly Madison's
Star*

*Grandmother's
Choice*

Excerpts from the Kennedy Reunion, June 1895,
The Jeffersonian Gazette, Lawrence, Kansas.

Margaret Ralston Kennedy

Forty years ago last Friday night a party of travelers camped at Hickory Point a few miles north of what is now Baldwin. The company had left Illinois one month previous in search of homes for themselves and children. They traveled in large covered wagons each drawn by four yoke of oxen. Traveling northward next morning, at the bow of the hill the beautiful valley of the Wakarusa burst upon their view, with its wide sweep of prairie land covered with luxuriant grass and flowers of every hue, and bordered and fringed by forest on the hill-sides and the banks of the creek.

The travelers with one accord decided that this should be their future home and at nightfall they were encamped on the banks of this stream a few rods above where we are now.

Here they lived for the first two weeks in their wagons and tents, before settling on their different claims. The majority of this company, twenty-three in number, belonged to the Kennedy family.

The survivors of that company with their families have met here today to celebrate the fortieth anniversary of their arrival.

As you talk of old times today, and look in each other's faces, you will not see the wrinkles with which toil and care have furrowed faces, nor the silver thread which father Time has given you, but rather you will remember each other as you were then—strong, stalwart men in the first flush of manhood, and rosy cheeked happy young mothers—scarcely realizing the hardships that lay before

85

you, yet pluckily determined to overcome then, whatever they might be.

The joyfulness of this reunion is saddened by the thought that all of the original number is not present. A mother, three sons and a daughter have fallen asleep but the memory of them lives—will ever remain with us. . . .

Mrs. Margaret Kennedy, the mother of the Kennedy family though somewhat advanced in years, came to this new country with her children and by her fortitude and courage which were always characteristic of her, sustained them when the days of trouble came.

It has been said of her that she was never known to speak an unkind word of any one. As a wife, mother and Christian, she fulfilled the highest ideal of an American woman. . . .

The men of Kansas during the days of '56 and of this locality in particular, striving to make her a free state had a very hard time, every hand was against him but God's.

The territorial government and national government were both in the hands of proslavery men, they were liable to be shot down in cold blood any day, their houses burned, crops destroyed, yet after all the blow seem to fall heavier on the women and children. Insufficient food, shelter and clothing sent scores of little children to their graves and weakened and enfeebled the constitution of many women.

It was the women's lot to remain at home, and endure that weary, weary waiting, while the men went forth to battle, all fearing that at any moment the husband or son would be brought home killed or wounded.

We children as we meet here today, cannot and never will be able to realize what you have passed through and what changes you have seen since those days. You have seen the system of slavery, which you here helped to make the first armed resistance to, shattered and obliterated. You have seen a territory grow into one of the grandest states in the union. You have seen the unbroken prairies become the garden of the world and the great American desert blossom as the rose. When once the oxen drew his weary load, you have seen the iron horse flying as if he had wings of the morning. You have seen greater chances in your generation than the next three will see.

86

Family Charts

Hugh Kennedy (1796-1845)
Margaret Jane Ralston (1800-1887)

children:
1. **Elizabeth A. Kennedy** (1821-1853)
   husband: **Abraham Liming** (1818-1881)
   1. Raymond Liming (1842-?)
   2. Virginia A. Liming (1844-?)
   3. Amanda J. Liming (1846-?)
   4. George N. Liming (1849-?)
   5. Matilda Liming (1852-?)

2. **William Bainbridge 'Bridge' Kennedy** (1822-1887)
   wife: **Elizabeth Jane Curless** (1829-1916)
   1. Margaret Jane Kennedy (1848-1849)
   2. Eugene Marshall Kennedy (1850-1923)
   3. Flora Martha Kennedy (1853-1886)
   4. Oscar Curless Kennedy (1855-1922)
   5. Josephine Kennedy (1857-1858)
   6. Ella Alice Kennedy (1860-1929)
   7. Lillie May Kennedy (1863-1928)
   8. Harvey Elmer Kennedy (1865-1865)
   9. Lucy Lena Kennedy (1867-1942)
   10. Effie Gertrude Kennedy (1871-?)

3. **Jonathan Ralston 'Joe' Kennedy** (1824-1883)
   1st wife: **Mary E. Neal** (1833-?)
   1. Oliver Jeff Kennedy (1851-1918)
   2nd wife: **Mary E. Jones** (? - ?)
   2. Matilda Kennedy (1854-?)
   3. Emma Kennedy (1855-1929)
   4. Katherine Kennedy (1857-?)
   5. Oran J. Kennedy (1859-?)

4. Sarah Jane 'Sed' Kennedy (1826-1902)
husband: **John Neal** (1801-1883)
1. Charles E. Neal (1856-1927)
2. Bainbridge Neal (1860-?)
3. Jesse Bell Neal (1862-?)
4. Randolph Neal (1868-?)

5. Zanetta Olivia 'Nettie' Kennedy (1828-1911)
husband: **William H. Curless** (1827-1909)
1. Joseph Warren Curless (1849-1913)
2. Sarah Catherine Curless (1851-?)
3. Frank Gilbert Curless (1853-1941)
4. Augusta Jane Curless (1855-1939)
5. Josephine Curless (1858-?)
6. Mary Curless (1860-?)
7. George Benson Curless (1863-1940)
8. Ella Alice 'Nellie' Curless (1865-1949)
9. Charles Van Pelt Curless (1868-1951)
10. Edmund K. Curless (1871-1931)

6. Catherine Blackburn 'Cate' Kennedy (1830-1909)
husband: **Collins Holloway** (1832-1905)
1. Rose D. Holloway (1852-1944)
2. Emery A. Holloway (1856-?)
3. Dora L. Holloway (1860-1936)
4. Scott R. Holloway (1862-1946)
5. Grant W. Holloway (1864-1902)
6. Margaret D. Holloway (1866-1946)
7. Thomas Kennedy Holloway (1869-1954)

7. Oliver Perry 'Scott' Kennedy (1831-1917)
1st wife: **Louise Price** (? - ?)
1. Jennie L. Kennedy (1855-1927)
2nd wife: **Martha M. Woodruff** (1842-1922)
2. Frank R. Kennedy (1862-1932)
3. Lizzie Belle Kennedy (1863-1944)
4. Melinda Kennedy (1867-1928)
5. Margaret M. 'Mollie' Kennedy (1871-1964)
6. Fred J. Kennedy (1875-?)

8. **Thomas Hamer Kennedy** (1832-1890)
wife: **Martha E. Nolan** (1841-1877)
   1. Thomas Hugh Kennedy (1861-1919)
   2. Martha Belle Kennedy (1862-?)
   3. Walter C. Kennedy (1866-?)
   4. Charles Kennedy (?-?)

9. **Leander Jackson 'Doc' Kennedy** (1835-1903)
wife: **Amanda Ellen Todd** (1841-1926)
   1. Isabelle Kennedy (1860-1860)
   2. Eva Lynn Kennedy (1861-1947)
   3. Elmer Hugh Kennedy (1863-1929)
   4. Charles Todd Kennedy (1866-1950)
   5. Harvey Leander Kennedy (1868-1937)
   6. Ida May Kennedy (1871-1873)
   7. Clarence Liming Kennedy (1874-?)
   8. Albert Rutherford Kennedy (1876-1969)
   9. Harry Ansil Kennedy (1881-1923)

10. **Joseph Warren Kennedy** (1837-1838)

11. **Mary Ann Kennedy** (1839-1839)

12. **Matilda M. Kennedy** (1840-1852)

13. **Salina F. Kennedy** (1841-1868)
husband: **Alonzo Hindman** (1840-1914)
   1. Charles Hindman (c. 1860-?)
   2. Capitola Hindman (c. 1862-?)
   3. Arthur Hindman (c. 1864-?)
   4. Harry Hindman (c. 1866-?)
   5. baby Hindman (1868-1868)

Michael B. Kennedy (1799-1847)
Hannah Rumery (1804-1850)

children:
1. **Moses Hopkins Kennedy** (1821-1878)
   wife: **Margaret Sraufe** (1823-1878)
   1. Michael W. Kennedy (1846-1925)
   2. Thomas Lafayette Kennedy (1848-?)
   3. Adam Wilson Kennedy (1854-?)
   4. Simon Bartholomew Kennedy (1857-?)
   5. William Sidney Kennedy (1859-1950)

2. **Mary Ann Kennedy** (1825-1881)
   1st husband: **Wilson J. Leonard** (1825-1852)
   1. Francis Marion Leonard (1846-?)
   2. Mahala Jane Leonard (1847-?)
   3. Amanda Leonard (1849-1851)
   4. George Wilson Leonard (1851-?)
   2nd husband: **Abraham Liming** (1818-1881)
   1. Elizabeth Liming (1856-?)
   2. Jaspar Liming (1859-?)
   3. Warren Liming (1860-?)
   4. twin? Walter Liming (1860-1860)
   5. Mary Ann Liming (1862-1919)
   6. Margaret Jane Liming (1866-?)

3. **no name Kennedy** stillborn (Jan 1828-1828)

4. **Sarah Thompson Kennedy** (Nov 1828-1849)
   husband: John Leonard

5. **twin- Elizabeth H. Kennedy** (Nov 1828-?)

6. **no name Kennedy** stillborn (1831-1831)

7. **William James Kennedy** (1832-1903)
   wife: **Lucinda Shields** (1839-1923)
   1. Alonzo Birk Kennedy (1858-1861)
   2. Mary Caroline Kennedy (1860-1861)
   3. Lizzie Jane Kennedy (1861-?)

4. Asa Dutton Kennedy (1863-1953)
5. Frank Hadley Kennedy (1865-1923)
6. John Howard Kennedy (1867-?)
7. Flora Martha Kennedy (1872-?)
8. Horace Elwood Kennedy (1879-?)

8. **Michael Washington Kennedy** (1835-1900)
wife: **Catherine Crouse** (1850-1945)
no children

9. **Hannah Caroline Kennedy** (1838-?)
husband: **Oliver P. Perkins** (1834-?)
1. J. Bradford Perkins (1860-?)
2. Edwin William Perkins (1862-?)
3. Leander A. Perkins (1866-?)
4. James Perkins (1868-?)
5. John Perkins (1870-?)
6. Lucinda Perkins (1874-?)

10. **John Alonzo Kennedy** (1841-1921)
1st wife: **Martha Mildred Strawn** (1849-1908)
1. John William Kennedy (1870-1870)
2. John Alonzo Kennedy Jr. (1872-1945)
3. Harrison Lee Kennedy (1883-1928)
2nd wife: **Mary C. Williamson** (1853-1921)

11. **Margaret Jane "Maggie" Kennedy** (1846-1882)
husband: **James Monroe Pieratt** (1844-1913)
1. Marion Robert Pieratt (1865-1933)
2. John Alonzo Pieratt (1867-1867)
3. James Monroe Pieratt Jr. (1870-1931)
4. William Ira Pieratt (1873-1964)
5. Martha Adeline Pieratt (1877-1948)
6. twin- Mary Caroline Pieratt (1877-1880)
7. Asa Burton Pieratt (1881-1882)

Joseph Warren Curless (1801-1851)
Lucy Hood (1808-1878)

children:
1. **John Washington Curless** (1825-1905)
   wife: **Mary Jane McIntire**

2. **William Henry 'Bill' Curless** (1827-1909)
   wife: **Zanetta Olivia Kennedy** (1828-1911)
   see children under Kennedys

3. **Elizabeth Jane Curless** (1829-1916)
   husband: **William Bainbridge Kennedy** (1822-1887)
   see children under Kennedys

4. **Edmund Curless** (1831-1894)
   wife: **Mary Newton**

5. **Joseph Curless Jr.** (1833-1877)
   wife: **Lorena Gould**

6. **Moses Lafayette 'Lafe' Curless** (1835-1885)
   wife: **Armintha McDaniels**

7. **Martha Curless** (1840-1845)

8. **Mary Melvina Curless** (1842-1914)
   husband: **James Prentiss**

9. **James K. Polk Curless** (1844-1870)
   wife: **Elizabeth Ann Ray**

10. **Sarah Jane Curless** (1847-1916)
    husband: **Edward Line**

11. **Thomas L. H. Curless** (1850-1880)

John W. Curless (?-?)
Phoebe Rumery (1804 -?)

children:
1. Tracy Curless (?-?)
2. James R. Curless (1825-1886)
3. Nancy Curless (1825-1873)
4. William Curless (?-?)
5. Mary Louise Curless (1832-1897)
6. Jonathan Jackson Curless (1835-1892)
7. Samuel H. Curless (1838-1916)

John Pieratt (1817-1868)
1st wife: **Deborah Goodpaster (1821-1859)**

children:
1. Levi Pieratt (1840-1840)
2. Belvard Pieratt (1841-1870)
3. James Monroe Pieratt (1844-1913)
4. Robert Letcher Pieratt (1846-1863)
5. Sarah Pieratt (1848-1903)
6. George Ann Pieratt (1850-1879)
7. Emma Pieratt (1853-1929)
8. John Franklin Pieratt (1855-1908)

2nd wife: **Nancy Shields** (1830-1863)
9. Joseph Pieratt (1860-1860)
10. Mary Pieratt (1861-?)

3rd wife: **Sarah Jane Wilkerson** (1846-1914)
11. William Graham Pieratt (1866-1933)
12. Jesse Pieratt (1868-1951)

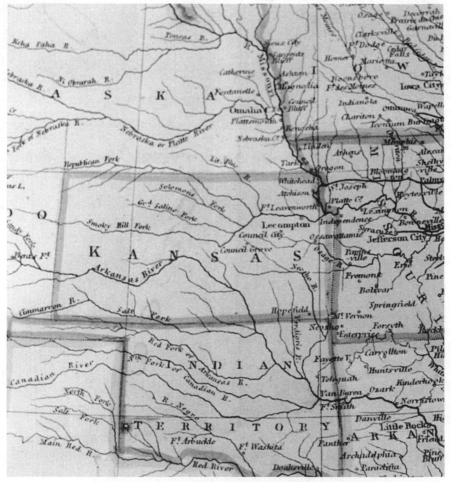

States crossed on trip (circa 1862 map)

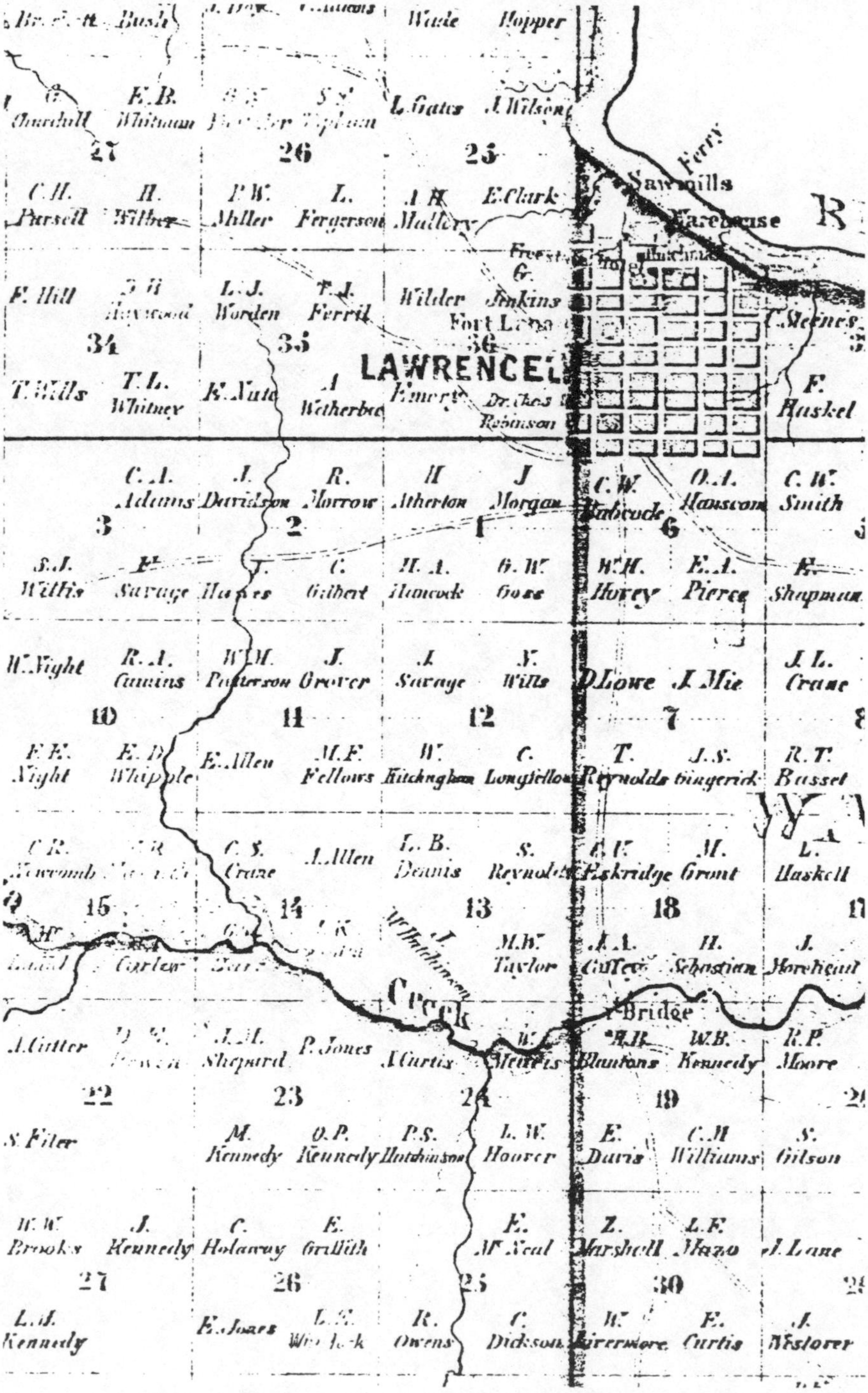

Part of Douglas County, Kansas Territory, 1857

IVER

Kalb

J. Jimison

34   35   36

J.W. Corel   J.W.T. Mathews   J.M'Gee   P.K. Nolan   P. Carter

H.L. Enos   Susanna M'Gee   J.J. M'Gee   Dobbins   T.S. Garvin   Seybort

5   4   3   2   1

J. Neal   James M'Gee   A.N. M'Gee   J. Anderson   L.G. Anderson

J. Neal   J. M'Farland   R. M'Farland   R. Samuel

FRANKLIN

8   9   J.S.   11   12

T. Seaton   H. Eggard   J. Epley   Wallace   S. Crane   J. Flora   Wakarosa

Wakarosa Camp   Fort

AKAROSA

Waller   K.B. Johnston   S. Crane   J.D. Herrington   McIniss   13

R.M. Wilkinson   J. Pierette   T.B. Smith   T. M'Farland   L.A. Prather   14   SEBAST

To Westport My   Anderson

A.D. Todd   J.E. Stuart   H. Dunbar   R. Irwin   J. Hogue

21   22   23   24

J. Ogden   H. Spalding   F.P. Vaughn   J.M. Still   N. Davidson

H.C. Burges N.W. Morgan   J. Derby   S. Ogden   E.A. London   E. Winslow

28   27   26   25

H.C. Burges N.W. Morgan   W. Jones   A. Flanders   M. Park   A.W. Maberly   C.J. Howe

House

Map compiled by J. Cooper Stuck

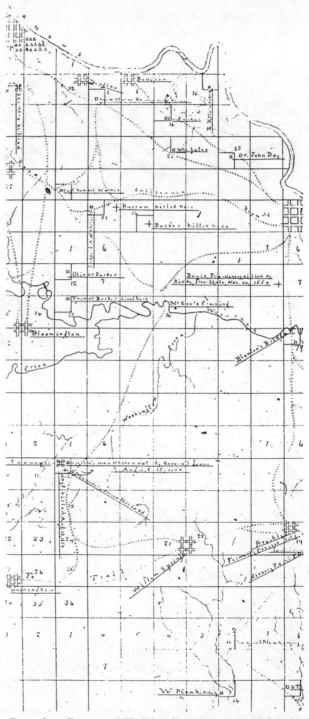

Douglas County, KT- Bleeding Kansas, 1854-60

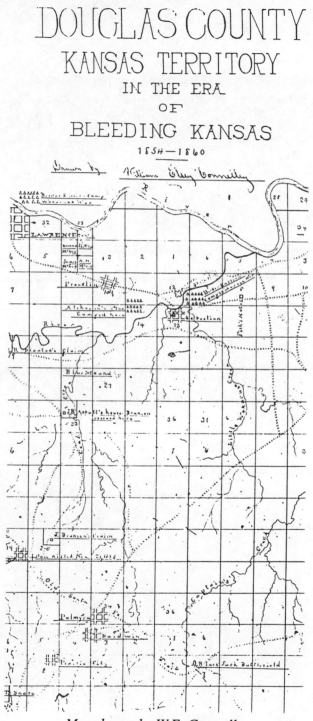

DOUGLAS COUNTY
KANSAS TERRITORY
IN THE ERA
OF
BLEEDING KANSAS
1854—1860

Map drawn by W.E. Connelly

Selected Bibliography

Andreas, A. T. *History of the State of Kansas*. Chicago: A. T. Andreas, 1883.

Brown, Dee. *The Gentle Tamers: Women of the Old Wild West*. Lincoln: University of Nebraska Press, 1981.

Brown, Robert L. *The Great Pikes Peak Gold Rush*. Caldwell, Idaho: The Caxton Printers, Ltd., 1985.

Collins, David R. *James Buchanan: 15th President of the United States*. Ada, Okla.: Garrett Educational Corporation, 1990.

Connelley, William Elsey. *A Standard History of Kansas and Kansans, Volume 1*. Chicago: Lewis Publishing Co., 1918.

————. *Quantrill and the Border Wars*. Cedar Rapids, Iowa: The Torch Press, 1910.

Davis, Kenneth S. *Kansas: A Bicentennial History*. New York: W. W. Norton & Company, Inc., 1976.

Fehrenbacher, Don E. *Prelude to Greatness: Lincoln in the 1850's*. Stanford, Calif.: Stanford University Press, 1962.

Gara, Larry. *The Presidency of Franklin Pierce*. Lawrence: University Press of Kansas, 1991.

Gleed, Charles S., ed. *The Kansas Memorial: A Report of the Old Settlers' Meetings held at Bismarck Grove, Kansas, September 15 and 16, 1879*. Kansas City, Mo.: Press of Ramsey, Millett and Hudson, 1880.

Graham, Lorenz. *John Brown: A Cry for Freedom*. New York: Thomas Y. Crowell Junior Books, 1980.

Greeley, Horace. *An Overland Journey from New York to San Francisco in the Summer of 1859*. New York: Alfred A. Knopf, Inc., 1864.

Hall, Carrie A., and Rose G. Kretsinger. *The Romance of the Patchwork Quilt in America*. Caldwell, Idaho: The Caxton Printers, 1935.

Ley, Willy. *Visitors from Afar: The Comets*. New York: McGraw-Hill Book Company, 1969.

Lilly, Judy Magnuson. *Voices from the Valley*. Salina, Kans., 1994.

Litter, Loren K. *Bleeding Kansas: The Border War in Douglas and Adjacent Counties*. Baldwin City, Kans.: Champion Publishing, 1987.

Rattenbury, Richard, and Thomas E. Hall. *Sights West: Selections from the Winchester Museum Collection*. Cody, Wyo.: Buffalo Bill Historical Center, 1981.

Rawley, James A. *Race and Politics: "Bleeding Kansas" and the Coming of the Civil War*. Philadelphia: J.B. Lippincott Company, 1969.

Sagan, Carl, and Ann Druyan. *Comet*. New York: Random House, 1985.

Sigelschiffer, Saul. *The American Conscience: The Drama of the Lincoln-Douglas Debates*. New York: Horizon Press, 1973.

Shea, John C. *Reminiscences of Quantrell's [sic] Raid upon the City of Lawrence, Kas.* Kansas City, Mo., 1879.

Stampp, Kenneth M. *America In 1857: A Nation on the Brink*. New York: Oxford University Press, 1990.

Thomas, Robert B. *The Old Farmer's Almanac for 1859*. Boston, Mass.: Hickling, Swan & Brewer, 1858.

U.S. Government Records, County and State, for Illinois, Ohio, and Kansas.

Zamonski, Stanley W., and Teddy Keller. *The '59ers: Roaring Denver in the Gold Rush Days*. Frederick, Colo.: Platte 'N Press, 1983.

Books by Linda K. Hubalek

the *Butter in the Well* series

Butter in the Well

Read the endearing account of Kajsa Svensson Runeberg, an immigrant wife who recounts how she and
her family built up a farm on the unsettled prairie.
Quality soft book • $9.95 • ISBN 1-886652-00-7
6 x 9 • 144 pages

Prärieblomman

This tender, touching diary continues the saga of
Kajsa Runeberg's family through her daughter,
Alma, as she blossoms into a young woman.
Quality soft book • $9.95 • ISBN 1-886652-01-5
6 x 9 • 144 pages
Abr. audio cassette • $9.95 • ISBN 1-886652-05-8
90 minutes

Egg Gravy

Everyone who's ever treasured a family recipe or
marveled at the special touches Mother added to her
cooking will enjoy this collection of recipes and wisdom from the homestead family.
Quality soft book • $9.95 • ISBN 1-886652-02-3
6 x 9 • 136 pages

Looking Back

During her final week on the land she homesteaded,
Kajsa reminisces about the growth and changes she
experienced during her 51 years on the farm. Don't
miss this heart-touching finale!
Quality soft book • $9.95 • ISBN 1-886652-03-1
6 x 9 • 140 pages

(continued on next page)

Butter in the Well note cards— Three full-color designs per package, featuring the family and farm.

Homestead note cards—This full-color design shows the original homestead.

Either style of note card —$4.95/ set. Each set contains 6 cards and envelopes in a clear vinyl pouch. Each card: 5 1/2 x 4 1/4 inches.

Postcards— One full-color design of homestead. $3.95 for a packet of 12.

the *Trail of Thread series*

Trail of Thread
Taste the dust of the road and feel the wind in your face as you travel with a Kentucky family by wagon trail to the new territory of Kansas in 1854.

Quality soft book • $9.95 • ISBN 1-886652-06-6
6 x 9 • 124 pages

Thimble of Soil
Experience the terror of the fighting and the determination to endure as you stake a claim alongside the women caught in the bloody conflicts of Kansas in the 1850s.

Quality soft book • $9.95 • ISBN 1-886652-07-4
6 x 9 • 120 pages

Stitch of Courage
Face the uncertainty of the conflict and challenge the purpose of the fight with the women of Kansas during the Civil War.
Quality soft book • $9.95 • ISBN 1-886652-08-2
6 x 9 • 120 pages

Planting Dreams Series

Drought has scorched the farmland of Sweden and there is no harvest to feed families or livestock. Taxes are due and there is little money to pay them.

But there is a ship sailing for America, where the government is giving land to anyone who wants to claim a homestead.

So begins a migration out of Sweden to a new life on the Great Plains of America.

Can you imagine starting a journey to an unknown country, not knowing what the country would be like, where you would live, or how you would survive? Did you make the right decision to leave in the first place?

Planting Dreams
Follow Charlotta Johnson and her family as they travel by ship and rail from their homeland in 1868, to their homestead on the open plains of Kansas.
Quality soft book • $9.95 • ISBN 1-886652-11-2
6 x 9 • 124 pages

Cultivating Hope
Through hardship and heartache Charlotta and Samuel face crises with their children and their land as they build their farmstead.
Quality soft book • $9.95 • ISBN 1-886652-12-0
6 x 9 • 124 pages

Harvesting Faith
The work and sacrifice of the family's first years on the prairie are reaped in the growth of the family, farm and community.
Quality soft book • $9.95 • ISBN 1-886652-13-9
6 x 9 • 112 pages

Order Form

Book Kansas!/Butterfield Books, Inc.
P.O. Box 407
Lindsborg, KS 67456-0407
1-800-790-2665 / 785-227-2707 / 785-227-2017, fax
www.bookkansas.com

SEND TO:

Name _____

Address _____

City _____

State _____ Zip _____

Phone # _____

❏ Check enclosed for entire amount payable to

   Butterfield Books

❏ Visa   ❏ MasterCard   ❏ Discover

Card # ⬚⬚⬚⬚ ⬚⬚⬚⬚ ⬚⬚⬚⬚ ⬚⬚⬚⬚

Exp Date ⬚⬚

Signature (or call to place your order) _____ Date _____

ISBN #	TITLE	QTY	UNIT PRICE	TOTAL
1-886652-00-7	Butter in the Well		9.95	
1-886652-01-5	Prarieblomman		9.95	
1-886652-02-3	Egg Gravy		9.95	
1-886652-03-1	Looking Back		9.95	
	Butter in the Well Series - 4 books		35.95	
1-886652-05-8	**Cassette:** Prarieblomman		9.95	
	Note Cards: Butter in the Well		4.95	
	Note Cards: Homestead		4.95	
	Postcards: Homestead		3.95	
1-886652-06-6	Trail of Thread		9.95	
1-886652-07-4	Thimble of Soil		9.95	
1-886652-08-2	Stitch of Courage		9.95	
	Trail of Thread Series - 3 books		26.95	
1-886652-11-2	Planting Dreams		9.95	
1-886652-12-0	Cultivating Hope		9.95	
1-886652-13-9	Harvesting Faith		9.95	
	Planting Dreams Series - 3 books		26.95	
			Subtotal	
			KS add 6.9% tax	
Shipping & Handling: per address ($3.00 for 1st book. Each add'l. book .50)				
			Total	

Retailers and Libraries: Books are available through Butterfield Books, Baker & Taylor, Bergquist Imports, Booksource, Checker Distributors, Ingram, Skandisk and Western International.

RIF Programs and Schools: Contact Butterfield Books for discount, ordering and author appearances.

About the Author

A door may close in your life but a window will open instead.

Linda Hubalek knew years ago she wanted to write a book someday about her great-grandmother, Kizzie Pieratt, but it took a major move in her life to point her toward her new career in writing.

Hubalek's chance came unexpectedly when her husband was transferred from his job in the Midwest to the West Coast. She had to sell her wholesale floral business and find a new career.

Homesick for her family and the farmland of the Midwest, she turned to writing about what she missed, and the inspiration was kindled to write about her ancestors and the land they homesteaded.

What resulted was the *Butter in the Well* series, four books based on the Swedish immigrant woman who homesteaded the family farm in Kansas where Hubalek grew up.

In her second series, *Trail of Thread*, Hubalek follows her maternal ancestors, who traveled to Kansas in the 1850s. These three books relive the turbulent times the pioneer women faced before and during the Civil War.

Planting Dreams, her third series, portrays Hubalek's great-great-grandmother, who left Sweden in 1868 to find land in America. These three books trace her family's journey to Kansas and the homesteading of their farm.

Linda Hubalek lives in the Midwest again, close to the roots of her writing career.

The author loves to hear from her readers. You may write to her in care of Butterfield Books, Inc., PO Box 407, Lindsborg, KS 67456-0407.